MOTION PICTURES:
MAKING
CINEMA MAGIC

INNOVATORS

MOTION PICTURES:
MAKING
CINEMA MAGIC

Gina De Angelis

The Oliver Press, Inc.
Minneapolis

The Oliver Press, Inc.
Charlotte Square
5707 West 36th Street
Minneapolis, MN 55416-2510

Library of Congress Cataloging-in-Publication Data
De Angelis, Gina.
    Motion pictures: making cinema magic / Gina De Angelis.
        p. cm. — (Innovators ; 11)
    Summary: Profiles eight inventors of motion-picture technology, including W. K. L.
Dickson, Auguste and Louis Lumière, Lee de Forest, Herbert Kalmus, Linwood Dunn,
Mike Todd, and Garrett Brown.
    Includes bibliographical references and index.
    ISBN 1-881508-78-1
    1. Cinematography—History—Juvenile literature. 2. Cinematographers—Biography—
Juvenile literature. 3. Cinematography—History—Juvenile literature.
4. Cinematographers—Biography—Juvenile literature. [1. Cinematography—History. 2.
Cinematographers. 3. Inventors.] I. Title. II. Series.

TR848.D43 2004
778.5'09—dc21
                                        2002041032
                                            CIP
                                            AC

ISBN 1-881508-78-1
Printed in the United States of America
10 09 08 07 06 05 04   8 7 6 5 4 3 2 1

CONTENTS

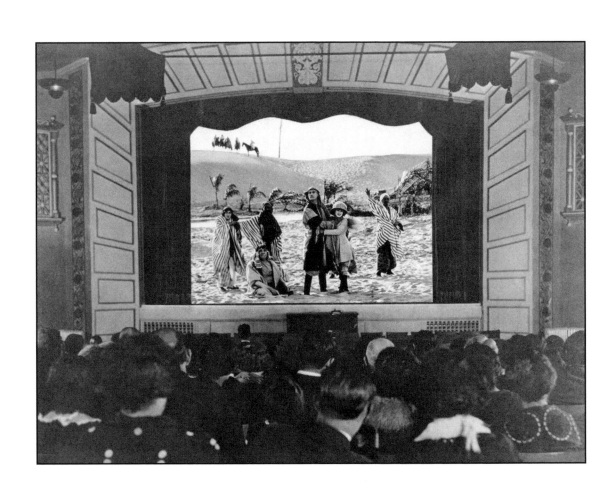

Pictures that Move

In the 2000 film *Crouching Tiger, Hidden Dragon*, people fly through the air atop a forest of bamboo trees during a spectacular martial-arts battle. In *The Matrix* (1999), bullets push slowly toward the hero, giving him a chance to duck. 1977's *Star Wars* features such carefully detailed spaceship battles that it is easy to imagine they're real. People around the world enjoy these and other illusions every day. They regularly pay as much as 10 dollars to crowd into large theaters and view new films in brilliant color on screens dozens of feet across, surrounded by elaborate sound systems that seem to put them in the middle of the action.

Only a little more than 100 years ago, people were astonished to see, on a tiny screen, a seconds-long, silent, black-and-white film showing a man sneezing. He was a real person! He moved! This was a technological marvel of the highest caliber. Audiences paid 25 cents for a peep at the new wonder

In the century since their invention, motion pictures have become a profitable business, a respected art form, and a major element of popular culture—as well as a constant source of technological innovation. Early audiences enjoyed the black-and-white silent film That Son of a Sheik *just as we might flock to a big-budget blockbuster today.*

that we now know simply as "movies." What seems so common to viewers today was a complex invention that had required many smaller discoveries before it could become a reality. Before innovators could even begin to try to record and play back pictures of motion, they needed to know how to record pictures at all. Motion pictures could not be developed until the invention of photography—the art of capturing real images of life.

People had been trying to transform light into fixed images since the 1500s, but it was not until 1826 that Joseph Nicéphore Niépce (1765-1833) took the first known photograph in history, *View*

The world's first photograph was taken at Joseph Nicéphore Niépce's Le Gras estate in Saint-Loup-de-Varennes, France.

from the Window at Gras. Niépce used a lens to collect and focus the sunlight that reflected off the objects around him. The light entered a dark box called a camera, where it struck a metal plate covered with light-sensitive chemicals. About eight hours of exposure to the sunlight bleached the chemicals to produce an image on the plate. Niépce called the result a "heliograph," or "sun drawing." Other inventors, notably Louis Jacques Mande Daguerre (1788-1851) and William Fox Talbot (1800-1877), developed different techniques that improved upon Niépce's work over the next three decades, and photography gradually achieved a standard form.

Compared to today's photography, the process used in the 1860s was complicated. A glass plate was coated with a wet emulsion (chemical mixture) and placed inside a large, heavy camera. When the photographer opened the shutter that covered the aperture, or opening, behind the camera's lens, light struck the glass plate and recorded a negative image (in which light and dark, as well as left and right, were reversed). The plate had to be removed from the camera immediately, before the emulsion dried, and soaked with developing chemicals that "fixed" the image permanently on the glass. Light could then be shone through the negative plate onto pieces of sensitized paper to produce photographs, known as positives. Photography quickly became both an art form and a scientific research tool, as well as a simple record of reality. It was even a form of popular entertainment; audiences flocked to "magic lantern" shows in which photographs were projected onto a screen.

lens: a curved piece of glass used to change the direction of light rays

A nineteenth-century magic lantern show. Probably invented by Dutch scientist Christian Huygens in about 1659, the magic lantern was the ancestor of the modern slide projector. It consisted of a light source that shone through pieces of glass painted with images and projected them on a wall or screen. Magic lantern exhibitions began traveling through Europe in the 1660s and remained popular for the next two centuries.

At around the same time, inventors introduced a variety of devices that made series of drawings appear to move. By presenting pictures of motion in sequence at a sufficient speed, they fooled the eye into accepting the images as movement. The trick worked because of a phenomenon called persistence of vision, which means that the human eye continues to "see" a picture for a split second even after it is gone. This is why, for example, our vision does not go dark every time we blink, or why we see the rotating blades of a fan as a single circle instead of as individual parts. All motion-picture technology is an optical illusion based on this quirk of human vision.

One of the earliest motion-picture toys was the Phenakistoscope (Greek for "deceitful view"), invented in 1832 by Joseph Antoine Ferdinand Plateau (1801-1883). It consisted of a cardboard disk mounted on a spindle. On the disk was a series of 16 drawings, each depicting a different phase of an object in motion, such as a turning wheel or a flying bird. The disk also had 16 slots around its edge. When a viewer held the device before a mirror, spun the disk, and looked through the slots, persistence of vision caused the drawings reflected in the mirror to appear to move.

A similar device that became a popular form of home entertainment was the Zoetrope, invented in 1834 by William George Horner (1786-1837). A cylinder with vertical slots was lined on the inside with a sequence of drawings on a long strip of paper, and when a viewer spun the cylinder and looked through the slots, the pictures seemed to move. Like the Phenakistoscope, it was a fun novelty, but neither produced true motion pictures. The movement they showed was disjointed and brief. No matter how beautiful or numerous the drawings were, they were still drawings, not real images of life. Only photography could record such images, but no one knew how to use it to capture motion—until an eccentric photographer named Eadweard Muybridge (1830-1904) was asked to prove a point.

In 1872, former California governor Leland Stanford, a racehorse owner, began arguing with a friend about whether all four hooves of a running horse ever leave the ground at once. The question

When people watch movies in a theater, the screen is actually blank for half of the time as the film moves from frame to frame and the projector's shutter opens and closes. But because of persistence of vision, their eyes view the images as continuous motion.

The Zoetrope had several advantages over the Phenakistoscope: it could be viewed by several people at once, the drum rotated longer and more evenly than the disk did, and the paper strips were cheap and easy to produce.

had nagged at observers for ages, because the naked eye cannot discern such rapid movement. Stanford hired Muybridge to figure it out. Muybridge photographed Stanford's famous horse, Occident, racing in Sacramento—but naturally, in the pictures Occident was a blur. Muybridge did not return to the problem until 1877, when he decided to line up 12 cameras, attach a wire to each one, and stretch the wires across a racetrack. He then had another of Stanford's horses, Sallie Gardner, run around the track. She broke the wires as she ran, tripping each

"Automatic electro-photographs" of Sallie Gardner and her rider, taken by Muybridge on June 19, 1878, in Palo Alto, California. Each image shows the horse moving about 27 inches forward.

camera's shutter and taking a rapid series of photographs. By 1879, Muybridge had perfected the system by adding another 12 cameras. Each picture captured the movement of 1/500 of a second, and viewed in the proper order, they showed the horse in motion. Stanford got his proof that a running horse, for a split second, has all four hooves off the ground. More importantly, Muybridge had hit upon a basic principle of motion pictures: a sequence of many still photographs can be viewed in quick succession to create the illusion of lifelike movement.

But Muybridge had created pictures of motion, not motion pictures. To advance the concept further, he invented the Zoopraxiscope, one of the first devices that projected moving images to be viewed by an audience. Muybridge developed his pictures around the edge of a round glass plate, then shone light through the glass plate and onto a screen. As the plate spun around, the images on the screen appeared to move. The invention was a hit when it was introduced in the 1880s, but the process was difficult, slow, and expensive. The heavy, fragile glass plate limited the number of images to only a few seconds of motion.

In 1885, real motion pictures became more possible when photographic pioneer George Eastman (1854-1932) introduced rolled-paper film. Instead of clumsy glass plates, photographers could now use a slim, relatively flexible material—paper coated with photographic chemicals. This film could hold a whole series of images in sequence, and it could be made as long as necessary. But paper,

Eadweard Muybridge continued photographing motion studies of animals, including dogs, deer, oxen, and birds. He also recorded men, women, and children performing actions such as leaping, wrestling, and somersaulting. More than 20,000 of these images were published in a book, *Animal Locomotion*, in 1887.

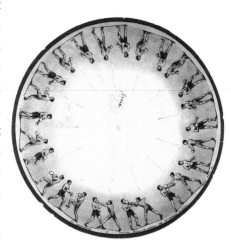

A Zoopraxiscope disk showing two men boxing

Rolled-paper film was only one of George Eastman's revolutionary photographic inventions. In 1880, he began marketing a new "dry" emulsion that was far more convenient than temperamental wet gelatin. In 1888, he introduced the small, inexpensive, easily operated Brownie camera. The Eastman Kodak Company he founded went on to produce a number of other innovations and is still a leading firm in film manufacturing and developing.

though better than glass, was not strong or flexible enough to be run through a device at the high speeds needed to record and view motion.

The solution lay in a cotton-like substance called nitrocellulose, which was derived from cellulose—a natural material from plant cells—treated with sulfuric and nitric acids. In 1868, John Wesley Hyatt (1837-1920) found that combining nitrocellulose with camphor produced a colorless material that he called celluloid. Celluloid was originally used as a substitute for ivory in products such as combs and billiard balls. But since it could be produced in thin, clear sheets that were both stronger and more flexible than paper, it was also ideal for photographic experiments.

In 1887, a clergyman named Hannibal Goodwin (1822-1900) applied for a patent on an invention he called "photographic pellicle," which was celluloid with an added light-sensitive emulsion for capturing images. Goodwin's patent was not granted for another 11 years, and in the meantime, George Eastman recognized the invention's value and set his chemists to work on it. An Eastman employee, Harry Reichenbach, filed for a patent on a substance similar to Goodwin's in 1889, and Eastman began to produce his own transparent roll film. This material would soon be used to record the first-ever motion pictures. All the necessary elements—from practical photographic methods to optical toys and motion studies—were in place, and the stage was set for someone to combine them.

Although many people strove to create the first motion pictures, the race was finally won by William Kennedy Laurie Dickson, an enterprising young employee of famous inventor Thomas Edison. In the 1890s, Dickson created the earliest devices for recording and viewing real motion pictures, establishing the basis for movies as we know them. From Dickson's work grew all the successful inventions that followed—including the Lumière brothers' motion-picture projector, Lee de Forest's sound-on-film recording system, Herbert Kalmus's color film processing, Linwood Dunn's special-effects technology, Mike Todd's wide screens, and Garrett Brown's moving camera. Together, these innovators shaped a new art form and a very lucrative industry.

Over the next century, motion pictures became part of modern society. Much like electricity, automobiles, and computers, they changed American and international culture. Film actors, directors, and studio chiefs became public figures as rich, famous, and powerful—or more so—than politicians and business tycoons. Movies even helped build a modern metropolis: the city of Los Angeles, which grew dramatically as a result of the burgeoning turn-of-the-century film industry. Motion pictures were once only a dream, pursued by obscure hobbyists who pushed the limits of nineteenth-century technology. This book will investigate how movies developed into a force to entertain, inform, influence, and bring magic to modern life.

In the early days of movies, sunlight was the only light strong enough for filming. Directors, producers, and actors began to migrate from New York to Southern California—in particular to a small village in the Los Angeles area called Hollywood—where warm, sunny weather allowed outdoor filming even in winter. By 1914, Hollywood was an established motion-picture town. Film industry workers there became known among locals as "movies," a term that was applied only later to the films themselves.

CHAPTER ONE

W. K. L. Dickson
and the Kinetograph and Kinetoscope

Menlo Park, New Jersey, was the home of a sprawling complex that was a buzzing hive of activity in the 1870s and 1880s: the laboratory of Thomas Alva Edison, perhaps the most famous American of his time. The "Wizard of Menlo Park" was known worldwide as the creator of the electric light bulb, the phonograph, and hundreds of other inventions. Edison had become wealthy and successful, but he still worked up to 90 hours a week—and he expected his assistants to work just as hard. Known as "muckers," a name that describes the slow, tedious process of invention, they built and tested new devices while helping Edison develop and refine his ideas. Edison assigned tasks to his muckers, who then could spend months or even years working on them. When a mucker built a successful device, Edison got the credit for the invention. It was, after all, his laboratory where the mucker worked, and his money that bought the supplies. The inspiration

phonograph: a machine that used a needle to play back sound recorded on a grooved, rotating cylinder or disk; invented by Thomas Edison in 1877

An assistant of Thomas Edison, William Kennedy Laurie Dickson (1860-1935) developed the first practical motion-picture camera and viewing machine, becoming one of the unsung heroes of film history. Here, Dickson (standing, left) poses with Edison (seated, center) and other employees after three straight days of work on an earlier invention, the phonograph (on table).

Muckers hard at work in Edison's laboratory in 1880

for the device was usually Edison's as well, though the design itself may have been the mucker's.

William Kennedy Laurie Dickson, a teenager in London in 1879, read about Edison in a newspaper and was intrigued by his inventions. Dickson sent him a telegram, offering to work in the labs at Menlo Park. On March 4, Edison replied: "I cannot increase my list of employees as I have concluded to close my works for at least 2 years, as soon as I have finished experiments with the electric light."

This was hardly a letter of encouragement. "In spite of this," Dickson later wrote, "I persuaded my mother and sisters to pull up stakes" and move to the United States. He took his resumé and references with him, planning to show them directly to Edison at his New York office. "My reception was unique," he later wrote. "'But I told you not to come, didn't I?' said Mr. Edison. I agreed, but told him I couldn't have done otherwise after reading about the work in which he was engaged. He watched my face while turning my testimonials over, and I had to remind him please to read them. He only replied, 'I reckon they are all right; you had better take your coat off and get to work.' I had won."

William Kennedy Laurie Dickson had been born in Minihic-sur-Ranse, France, to British parents in August 1860. His father, James Dickson, was an artist, and his mother, Elizabeth Kennedy-Laurie, was known for her intellect and her musical talent. James Dickson died when his son was a young boy, but not much else is known about William's youth. By the time he was 19, the Dicksons had moved from France to England, and William had become an avid amateur photographer.

W. K. L. Dickson's hobby soon gave Edison an idea of what to do with his new mucker. Edison wanted to combine his recently invented phonograph with an equivalent machine for sight, so that the sounds of the phonograph would be accompanied by moving pictures produced by another device. After several years of proving his talents in other Edison enterprises, Dickson was assigned to manage this new project. When Edison's new laboratory in West

Thomas Edison (1847-1931) with his phonograph in 1888. A few months later he declared, "I am experimenting upon an instrument which does for the Eye what the phonograph does for the Ear, which is the recording and reproduction of things in motion, and in such a form as to be . . . cheap, practical and convenient."

Orange, New Jersey, was completed in 1887, Dickson picked two rooms as his offices and set to work.

Dickson began, as most inventors do, by noting what others had developed. He was interested in Eadweard Muybridge's Zoopraxiscope, one of the first systems to project moving images onto a screen. In addition, he studied Étienne-Jules Marey's new Chronophotograph, a portable device that was something like a photographic gun. Its "barrel" contained a shutter that opened to record sequential images on a round glass disk coated with light-sensitive chemicals. Both inventions worked for the purposes of their inventors, who wanted to study motion by slowing it down and recording it step by step. Dickson's goal, however, was to reproduce motion exactly as it appeared in reality; the pictures of life had to move as fast as life itself did. No existing methods could take enough pictures fast enough to play back later at high speed.

Nor would the glass plates used in photography help Dickson. They were too small, heavy, and fragile to record motion. Since Edison had originally envisioned a device similar to the phonograph, which recorded sound onto wax cylinders, Dickson's first experimental motion-picture cameras recorded spiraling patterns of tiny images onto metal or glass drums coated in a homemade light-sensitive emulsion. But the process was clumsy and frustrating, and he kept looking for a better way.

emulsion: a mixture of chemicals; in photography, a mixture of light-sensitive chemicals applied to film

THE BREAKTHROUGH

After a long night of trial and error, Dickson later recalled, "My second batch of emulsion was light struck [exposed to light too early and ruined], owing to the night-watchman's bursting in at 2 A.M., which so disgusted me that I just slotted the aluminum drum and wrapped a sheet of . . . stiff sensitized celluloid over it." Instead of recording images on the emulsion-coated drum, he now recorded them on the flexible, transparent celluloid, which produced sharp pictures and was easier to use and develop. To fit on a square sheet, however, the images had to be almost microscopic. Dickson decided that what he needed was "to get away from drums, disks, etc., and a hopelessly limited number of pictures."

Dickson began experimenting with taking pictures on narrow strips of celluloid about 14 inches long. Since he no longer wanted to turn the film on a rotating cylinder, he needed another way to advance it smoothly to take each successive picture. If the images jerked back and forth, froze, or skipped ahead, the illusion of motion would be lost. To solve this problem, Dickson's lab assistant William Heisse fashioned an advancing device of clawed gears called sprockets. The strips of film were perforated, or edged with rows of evenly spaced holes. The sprockets fit neatly into the holes, and as the gears turned they pulled the film along with them. The regular spacing ensured that the film advanced from a reel—a wheel-like device around which the strip of film was wrapped—to another reel, at a certain steady rate.

Many years later, film scholars discovered that a system of sprockets and perforations had been used before Dickson—by a French inventor, Augustin Le Prince. Le Prince developed his motion-picture device in 1889 and applied for patents in several countries. Unfortunately, he disappeared, along with all his papers and luggage, in September 1890. He was presumed dead by 1897.

frame: one individual image on a strip of motion-picture film

This advancing system was synchronized with the camera shutter, the device that alternately opened and closed the aperture (opening) behind a camera lens. When the shutter was open, light would pass through the lens to the film, recording an image; when the shutter was closed, no light would reach the film. Dickson employed a stop-motion mechanism to hold each frame of unexposed film in front of the open camera shutter for a fraction of a second, exposing the film and recording the image. This made it possible to photograph each image separately; if there had been continuous movement, the viewer would see only a blur. It also allowed a standard rate of film advance, keeping the pictures from slowing down or speeding up.

The first experimental films worked well, and Dickson and his fellow viewers were so excited that no one minded having to thread the short strips of film through the machine over and over again. But they knew they needed a longer format. Even by joining several strips together, they could achieve a maximum length of just 40 inches—enough to record only a few seconds of motion. Dickson found a solution in late 1888, when he attended an exhibit of George Eastman's celluloid film at the New York Camera Club. Impressed, Dickson went to Rochester, New York, the next day to meet the man behind the great Eastman Company. Eastman gave Dickson some 35-millimeter-wide film samples and told him they could be produced in 50-foot lengths. Through the coming months, Eastman's laboratory worked to refine the film to meet Dickson's needs.

By 1889, Dickson had developed a working motion-picture camera, the Kinetograph. Two years later, he also completed a viewing machine, the Kinetoscope. (Both devices got their names from ancient Greek: *kineto-* means "motion," *-scope* means "examine," and *-graph* means "drawing" or "picture.") The Kinetoscope did not use the Kinetograph's stop-motion technology; instead, a small motor ran the film continuously around a series of spools. The viewer looked through a peephole in the large wooden cabinet that housed the machine, and light from an electric bulb shone through the film to illuminate the pictures as they moved past.

One of the earliest Kinetograph films—the first motion picture ever copyrighted—featured an

An early version of Dickson's motion-picture camera. The strips of film ran horizontally across the back; the disk with holes in it rotated to block and admit light to the lens behind it at regular intervals. Dickson later switched to a setup in which the film ran vertically.

The Kinetograph as it appeared by 1912 (right), and the Kinetoscope (below) with its cabinet open to reveal the reels of film within

Edison lab assistant sneezing. *Fred Ott's Sneeze* was black and white, silent, and only about five seconds long. Compared to today's motion pictures, the movement looks jerky and too fast, and the image is grainy. Yet to people who had never seen motion pictures, it was magic. Edison and Dickson rushed to make more films that would show off the value of their inventions. While waiting for his patents to be granted on the Kinetograph and Kinetoscope, Edison approved the building of the first film studio. This tar-paper-covered building on the laboratory grounds at West Orange became known as the "Black Maria," from a slang term for a police wagon, which it resembled. The roof cranked open to admit sunlight, and the entire structure rotated on a track to follow the sun. There, assisted by William Heisse, Dickson filmed—and sometimes appeared in—the world's first true motion pictures.

"I had to do my best to secure attractive subjects for the Kinetoscopes," Dickson later wrote. "No earthly stage has ever gathered within its precincts a more incongruous crew of actors." He later listed some of the vaudeville acts he filmed: "Trick Dog Teddy and other Dog and trick Cats; Madame Bertoldi, contortionist; . . . Colonel Cody's (Buffalo Bill) Shooting Skill; Colonel Cody and his Sioux Indians; . . . Sandow in Feats of Strength; Texan Cowboy Throwing Lassos; . . . Mexican Knife Thrower; . . . Japanese Dancers." In 1894 alone, Dickson made more than 75 Kinetograph films (each between 16 and 60 seconds long).

Several frames of film from Fred Ott's Sneeze

Dickson took this picture of the Black Maria, with its roof open and employees standing by, in late 1894 or early 1895. The track on which the building turned is visible in the foreground.

Once his patents were granted in 1893, Edison sold coin-operated Kinetoscope machines for about $250 to $300 each, along with the films to show in them. The first "Kinetoscope parlor," a carpeted, saloon-like room with rows of Kinetoscopes lined up along a wall, opened in April 1894 on Broadway in New York City. This parlor was followed quickly by others across the United States and overseas. Thousands of people lined up to see Edison's latest marvel. They paid 25 cents, peered through an eyepiece, and, for the first time in their lives, got to see real motion pictures.

THE RESULT

Edison had hoped the Kinetoscope machines would be a moneymaking venture for his laboratory. Apparently, though, he lacked confidence in the devices, because he did not file for an international patent. Edison's neglect made it legal to copy his motion-picture technology outside the United States. Certainly, the Kinetoscope had drawbacks: it could be viewed by only one person at a time, and within a few short years the magic of watching one-minute films of a quick dance or a performing bear wore thin. The price of admission dropped to ten cents, then five (hence, Kinetoscope parlors and other early movie houses became known as "nickelodeons"). In the end, Edison sold only about 900 Kinetoscopes.

W. K. L. Dickson, far from satisfied with the Kinetograph and Kinetoscope, wanted to develop a projection device that would allow many people to watch a film at the same time. Edison, however, was content to earn money by selling new films for Kinetoscopes. He refused to allow Dickson to experiment with film projection—particularly if that meant the Kinetoscope would become obsolete. Edison demanded that Dickson continue devoting his time to making new Kinetoscope films. Dickson resented this waste of his talents, and he began investigating projection on his own.

In 1894, Dickson was contacted by the Latham family—brothers Otway and Gray and their father, Woodville—who had just opened a Kinetoscope parlor and wanted to show films of prizefights. Dickson

patent: government recognition that an invention belongs to a particular inventor, which gives the inventor the sole right to produce and sell the invention for the duration of the patent

and the Lathams teamed up to film several fights, but because Kinetograph film was so short, they had to record each round separately. They experimented with making longer films, eventually creating a device called the Eidoloscope that could record and project an eight-minute, uninterrupted fight. One of the reasons Kinetograph films were so short was that the longer a strip of film was, the more likely it was to break as it was pulled through the machine. The Lathams solved this problem simply: they put a loop in the film between each reel and the lens. The "Latham loop" took pressure off the film and reduced breakage, allowing unlimited recording length.

In 1895, an amateur inventor named Thomas Armat incorporated the loop into his own projection device for Kinetograph films. Dickson learned of the successful invention and may even have convinced Armat to sell the rights to Edison. At around this time, however, the long-developing rift between Dickson and Edison came to a head. Although the details of the quarrel are unknown, Dickson probably felt that Edison was an ungrateful and oppressive boss. For his part, Edison later wrote that Dickson had "double X" (doublecrossed) him, apparently by moonlighting on other inventions. In April 1895, Dickson left Edison's employment.

Edison bought Armat's device outright, and the terms of the sale allowed him to manufacture it as his own invention. (A small plate on the back of the projector credited Armat as the "designer.") Edison named the projector Vitascope (*vita-* means "life") and exhibited it in New York in April 1896.

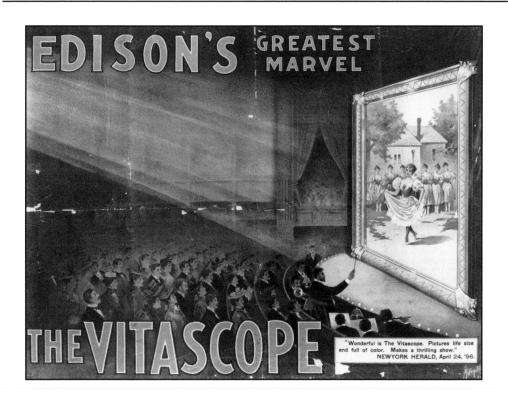

"Wonderful is The Vitascope. Pictures life size and full of color. Makes a thrilling show."
NEW YORK HERALD, April 24, '96.

Using his considerable fame and fortune, he pushed Vitascope sales. He was still the main supplier of motion pictures in the U.S., but his projector faced heavy competition as other inventors rushed to create machines that showed the popular Kinetograph films. Some went even further and invented their own motion-picture systems.

By the end of 1895, Dickson and several partners in New York City were working to develop new motion-picture devices that would not infringe on Edison's patents. They started a company called the K. M. C. D. Syndicate, after the initials of its founders, but soon changed the name to "American

An advertisement for Edison's Vitascope shows a rapt audience watching a film. Although motion pictures did not yet have sound, musicians provided live accompaniment.

Mutoscope & Biograph Company" to better represent their products. The first of these was the Mutoscope, a peep-show-type device in which a sequence of photographs was arranged on a drum that rotated when the viewer turned the handle. The Biograph, invented in 1896, was a combination motion-picture camera and projector that used 70-millimeter film—twice the width of Edison's—to increase the picture sharpness. With this invention, Dickson and his associates began to film "entertainments" to sell. Since the company had only one camera at first, many early Biograph films were shot by Dickson himself.

As Dickson's business grew, it phased out the Mutoscope and became known simply as "Biograph." Biograph became Edison's main American competitor and employed many of the early movie industry's most illustrious stars. Dickson, however, left the company before it gained such prestige. In 1897, he returned to England to help expand Biograph's overseas operations, but he eventually tired of film and began working as an electrical engineer. Dickson stayed in England for the rest of his life, dying on September 28, 1935.

The number of companies producing motion-picture equipment and films continued to increase in the early twentieth century. But Edison still dominated the movie industry, and most projectors were designed to show his company's films. Even Biograph switched to 35mm film in 1904 to make its products more marketable. With the Kinetograph, Edison and Dickson had clearly set the standard for

Biograph's famous alumni included directors Mack Sennett (who later created the Keystone Kops and produced the first Charlie Chaplin films) and Edwin S. Porter (who had previously made the well-known film *The Great Train Robbery* while working for Edison), as well as star actors Lillian Gish and Mary Pickford. D. W. Griffith, at the time a struggling writer and actor, got his start in movies at Biograph in 1908. After learning his trade by directing about 450 short films for Biograph, Griffith went on to become one of the greatest early American directors with films such as *The Birth of a Nation* (1915) and *Intolerance* (1916).

motion-picture technology from that time forward: today, 35mm film is still perforated, advanced by sprockets, and illuminated by an electric light bulb. For decades, it was Edison who was credited as the inventor of motion pictures. Eventually, however, Dickson's vital part in developing movie technology became more widely recognized. The Film 100, a 1998 list of the 100 most influential people in motion pictures, listed Edison as the 10th most important figure in film history. William Kennedy Laurie Dickson was the first.

After leaving the United States, Dickson used the Biograph camera to document the Boer War in South Africa. He also traveled around Europe filming dignitaries such as Pope Leo XIII and events such as Queen Victoria's Diamond Jubilee celebration.

CHAPTER TWO

Auguste and Louis Lumière and the Cinematographe

Lumière, the French word for "light," seems a fitting name for a family who helped create an art form out of the scientific use of light. Claude-Antoine Lumière was a painter who turned to the new art of photography just as its popularity bloomed. His sons, Auguste and Louis Lumière, would take photography and move it into its future: motion pictures. For their invention of the first practical device that could film, print, and project moving images, the Lumière brothers became famous as "the fathers of cinematography."

The father of the fathers of cinematography, Claude-Antoine Lumière, was born in 1840 in southeastern France, the son of a winemaker. After being orphaned when his parents died of cholera, he was apprenticed to a Paris sign painter named Auguste Constantin in 1855. Before the age of 20, Antoine had become a skillful painter and married Jeanne-Josephine Costille. Their first son, Auguste,

Motion pictures moved closer to the form we know today when Auguste (left; 1862-1954) and Louis (1864-1948) Lumière invented a projector that could show a movie to an entire audience at once.

Antoine Lumière (1842-1911)

Instead of being coated with a wet emulsion that had to be used immediately before it dried, Ètiquette Bleue was a dry plate. Although Louis Lumière was not the first to use this technique, his dry plates were much more sensitive than previous ones.

was born in the town of Besançon on October 19, 1862; his brother Louis followed on October 5, 1864. In 1870, the Lumières moved to Lyon, where Antoine opened a photography studio. Antoine and Jeanne-Josephine had several other children over the years: daughters Jeanne, Juliette, and France, and a son named Edouard.

Auguste and Louis grew up influenced by their artistic father, who encouraged his sons in their education. Both Auguste and Louis attended La Martinière, the largest technical school in Lyon. Auguste was trained in engineering; Louis enjoyed visual arts but was gifted in science as well. At age 17, Louis invented a new, faster, and easier kind of photographic plate called "Ètiquette Bleue" ("Blue Label"). The invention came at the right time—just as photographic portraits grew more popular with middle-class families—and the Lumières earned a fortune making and selling the plates. Auguste also joined the family business, and the two brothers all but ran the company by 1882. When the demand grew too great for the Lumières to continue making the plates themselves, they opened a factory in the nearby suburb of Monplaisir. Lumière and Sons soon employed 300 workers and manufactured 15 million photographic plates per year. In addition to their scientific curiosity, the Lumière brothers now had the wealth to invest in new projects.

The Lumière family members' closeness to one another and to friends resulted in a remarkable set of marriages. In 1893, three Lumière siblings married three offspring of Alphonse Winckler, a brewer who was a close friend of Antoine's. While their sister Juliette married Jules Winckler, Auguste married Marguerite and Louis married Rose. (Ten years later, France Lumière would marry another Winckler son, Charles.) In 1894, both Auguste and Louis were blessed with baby daughters, named Andrée and Suzanne respectively. The change in the brothers' personal lives that year was matched by a turning point in their professional lives.

During a trip to Paris, Antoine Lumière saw Thomas Edison's Kinetoscope, a machine for viewing motion pictures. Antoine obtained a small piece of film to show to his sons and told them, "This is what you should be doing. Edison is making a fortune selling this." Louis examined the Kinetoscope and the Kinetograph—the device that filmed the pictures used in Kinetoscopes—and discussed them at length with his brother. They realized they could improve on Edison's machines. For example, Louis noted, the sharpness of the moving images could be much better, and the illumination was "feeble." At several hundred pounds, the Kinetograph was so big and heavy that it made filming clumsy. And most importantly, the Kinetoscope could only be seen by one viewer at a time. It would be far more efficient, the Lumières believed, if films could be projected onto a wall or screen in a darkened room, where they could be viewed by hundreds of people at once.

Watching films on a Kinetoscope required the viewer to hunch over and peer into a peephole. (This Kinetoscope was equipped with sound, heard through headphones.)

THE BREAKTHROUGH

Auguste Lumière liked to tell people, in later years, that his brother invented the cinema in a single night. The comment eventually led to misunderstanding about who deserved the credit; actually, the brothers worked together harmoniously on most projects. And the Lumières could not solve all their difficulties overnight. Auguste's remark referred to Louis's insomnia, which was caused by severe headaches. One night, unable to sleep, he came up with a solution to the problem of film advancement.

The Kinetoscope images were dim and blurry because they ran continuously, allowing the eye to see them for only a very short period of time. In a flash of inspiration, Louis realized that this problem could be solved by adapting technology from the sewing machine, which used an intermittent stitching system. This device fed the fabric into the machine and then held it still long enough to sew a stitch. In a film machine, a claw mechanism could be used to dig into the perforations, pull the film forward, and then stop it for an instant in front of the lens so that it could be fully illuminated and clearly viewed. If the stopping and starting occurred fast enough, it would create an illusion of continuous movement. The stickiest problem solved, the brothers moved forward quickly on their new invention.

In 1895, the Lumières filed a patent on a single machine that could photograph negative films, print positives, and project the positives onto a screen. This device, which the brothers dubbed the

negative: a film image that shows light and dark, and right and left, reversed; a camera records a negative, and then positive prints are developed from it

positive: a photograph or film produced from a negative that shows light and dark, and right and left, as seen in reality; also called a print

Cinematographe, was compact and streamlined in design. Contained within a small, square wooden housing, it weighed less than 11 pounds. Because it was powered by hand-cranking rather than electricity, there was no need for the large, heavy batteries required by the Kinetograph. At about the size of an ordinary photographic camera of the time, it was easy to use in nearly any location. Another advantage to the Cinematographe was its use of film. The Edison devices ran 48 frames of film per second, but the Lumières' ran only 16. This reduced the amount (and, therefore, the cost) of film, while causing less wear and tear on the machine.

Like the Kinetograph and Kinetoscope, the Cinematographe took its name from the ancient Greek words for "motion" and "picture."

The Cinematographe, opened to reveal its hand-cranking mechanism

An early viewer of La Sortie des Usines Lumière *described the film: "As the whistle blew, the factory doors were thrown open and men, women, and children came trooping out. Several of the employees had bicycles which they mounted outside the gate, and rode off. A carryall, which the Lumières keep to transport those who live at a distance from the factory, came dashing out in the most natural manner imaginable."*

The brothers' next step was to create films for their device to show. Running less than 60 feet in length, the Lumière films were brief, but—thanks to the brothers' background in artistic photography—less haphazardly put together than Edison's earliest films had been. The Lumières demonstrated their first complete film, as well as a few experimental color photographs, to members of the Society for the Encouragement of National Industry on March 22, 1895, in Paris. The film was titled *La Sortie des Usines Lumière (Workers Leaving the Lumière Factory)*. It was as simple as its title suggests, but the audience was amazed.

An engineer named Jules Carpentier who had attended the showing was so impressed that he offered to mass-produce the Cinematographe in his factory. Throughout the summer and autumn, Carpentier and the Lumières worked on perfecting the device. The brothers also filmed more than 60 everyday scenes, including Auguste and his wife, Marguerite, feeding their baby daughter, Andrée, in *La Répas de Bébé (Baby's Lunch)*. And they continued to arrange private viewings for scientists, photographers, and reporters. After each one, the astonished attendees eagerly wrote articles about the Lumière Cinematographe, making the device famous even before its official debut.

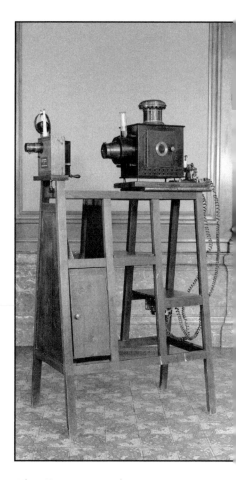

The Cinematographe set up for projection

The first demonstration of motion pictures that was open to the public took place in Paris on December 28, 1895, before a paying audience of about 35 people. The Lumière brothers were not present; instead, their father hosted the event. It was held in the Salon Indien, a jungle-decorated lounge in the basement of the Grand Café on Boulevard des Capucines. Admission was one franc per person. Although the program lasted less than 30 minutes, word spread quickly. One family friend later said, "What I remember as being typical was some passer-by sticking his head round the door, wanting to know what on earth the words Cinematographe Lumière could possibly mean. Those who took the plunge and entered soon reappeared looking astonished. They'd come back quickly with a few friends. . . . By afternoon, people were queuing [lining up] a quarter of a mile away."

A frame from L'arrivé d'un Train en Gare

Legend has it that the first Lumière films had viewers literally jumping from their seats. One, *La Mer (The Sea)*, supposedly caused people in the front row to dodge away in fear of getting wet. Another, *L'arrivé d'un Train en Gare (Arrival of a Train at a Station)*, started with a train tiny in the distance, approaching the camera from a diagonal angle—almost head-on. Some members of the audience reportedly jumped back as if they were about to be run over. Whether or not this story is true, filming the train's approach from an angle rather than from

the side made it noteworthy. Historians cite the film as the first use of camera placement to create dramatic tension.

The 35-person audience at the first showing became 300 people, then 2,500 per day in the following weeks. Although the Lumières were now showing their films 20 times daily, Louis believed the popularity of the exhibitions would fade. "It'll last six months or more," he told his assistants. In January 1896, Carpentier delivered the first order of factory-produced Cinematographes. The Lumière family, despite outrageously lucrative offers, initially refused to sell the machines. Wanting to protect their invention from copying and ensure that the films were shown at a high level of quality, they leased out a package that included the device itself, films, and two Lumière staff members (a projectionist and a box-office assistant). Cinematographes were not sold to the public until the following year.

To capitalize on their fame while they could, the Lumière family opened theaters especially for their Cinematographe films. By June 1896, there were "cinemas"—as they became known—in Berlin, Brussels, London, and New York, as well as in Paris and Lyon. The Lumières sent cameramen to 31 different countries to film new motion pictures for the cinemas. Within 10 years, they would produce 1,425 films. Yet despite all this activity, the brothers were still convinced their device was merely a passing fad. Louis famously said in 1896 that "the cinema is an invention without any commercial future." Events soon proved otherwise.

Louis Lumière films a scene with the Cinematographe.

THE RESULT

Thanks to the photography business, the Lumières were already well off when they entered the motion-picture race. But the Cinematographe gave them wealth far beyond their expectations. It also threw them into aspects of motion pictures they had not expected. They had invented the machine that was the seed from which the film industry grew, but their achievement was more than technological. They also developed techniques for using that machine; they were artists as well as scientists.

Some film historians see the birth of narrative film in the Lumières' work. While other early films featured simple motion of people or animals, several Lumière films told stories. *L'Arroseur Arrosée (The Sprinkler Sprinkled)*, for example, featured a gardener watering a lawn. Suddenly the water stopped; behind him, a boy had stepped on the hose. The gardener looked into the nozzle, confused. The boy stepped off the hose, and water blasted the gardener in the face. Most of the Lumières' films, however—like the film of the train's arrival—are best described as documentaries recording everyday events.

The Lumières showed their films at the 1900 Universal Exhibition in Paris on an enormous screen 69 feet wide and 49 feet high, which could be viewed

An advertisement for the Cinematographe shows audiences enjoying L'Arroseur Arrosée.

by an audience of 25,000. The screen was dipped in water before each showing to make it more reflective and thus increase the brightness of the projected image. Louis added a condensing device to the Cinematographe (basically a round glass flask full of water, which also served as a cooling system) that would help gather and focus the light as it shone onto the screen. He also experimented with a camera that used film almost twice as wide as the standard 35 millimeters, making it easier to project clear, large images. Unfortunately, this was not finished in time for the exhibition, and the Lumières had to make do with 35mm film.

The exhibition was a success, and Louis went on to invent a device called the photorama, which used 12 lenses to project a huge image onto a curved screen. But the Lumières soon lost interest in the large-screen project and turned back to photography. Worried about the safety hazard of flammable celluloid, they introduced nonflammable film made from acetate in 1909. Louis continued the brothers' long-standing experiments with color photography. Between 1903 and 1907, he developed Autochrome, a reliable process for making color pictures that was not improved on for many years.

Auguste, meanwhile, was interested in X-ray technology, which had been invented in the 1890s. A pioneer in the field, he was one of the first people to X-ray a fractured bone. In 1914, he was named the head of the radiology department of a major hospital in Lyon. During World War I, Auguste paid for the X-ray treatment of all the patients at the hospital,

Celluloid film was so flammable that it would often ignite in factories, in projectors, or even while in storage. "Safety film" made of cellulose acetate—which had the same properties as celluloid but was less volatile—was first developed in the United States by George Eastman in 1908. Acetate film became standard by 1948, and in 1950 the Eastman Kodak Company won an Academy Award for its invention.

In the Autochrome process, a glass plate was coated with grains of potato starch mixed with red, green, and blue dyes. A black-and-white negative was exposed through the coated glass plate, and the result was a color picture.

which cost him more than 200,000 francs. (His generosity during the war was matched by Louis, who set up and paid for a 100-bed hospital.) Auguste even invented a helpful wartime device that is still in use today: the catalytic heater that enables airplane engines to start in freezing weather.

The Lumières suffered a number of personal tragedies during the 1910s and 1920s. Their father died of a brain hemorrhage in 1911, and their mother died in 1915. They lost their youngest brother, Edouard, in World War I in 1917, and a year later, influenza killed Auguste's 24-year-old daughter, Andrée. In 1923, Louis's wife, Rose, passed away; two of the Lumière sisters, Juliette and France, died a year later, and in 1926, sister Jeanne also died.

Despite these losses, the family remained close and the brothers continued their valuable work. They were granted nearly 350 patents and wrote almost 250 articles. In the 1930s, Auguste published a medical textbook called *Horizons of Medicine*; his brother was busy remaking the famous train film in three dimensions. Both men continued working until their health prohibited it. Louis died at age 83 on June 6, 1948. Auguste, at 91, died on April 10, 1954.

three-dimensional (3-D): images that appear to have depth, as well as height and width; 3-D motion pictures seem to emerge from the screen toward the audience

The Lumières' Cinematographe was a product of such quality that the surviving machines are still in perfect working order today. Yet the brothers are known not only as the inventors of a device, but also as the pioneers who gave a new medium its name. In honor of their innovation, films became known as cinema, and the art and science of making motion pictures is still called cinematography.

CHAPTER THREE

Lee de Forest and Optical Sound

In the early days of film, there was silence. Motion pictures had no dialogue, no sound effects, and no music. Audiences could be raucous: they ate noisy snacks like nuts, talked, sang, and even shouted at the screen. Any necessary dialogue was provided by occasional "titles" that interrupted the action. These words, printed in white letters on a black background, were translated into other languages when a film was to be sold overseas. But the fewer the titles, the better; many people in the 1900s and 1910s could not read anyway. Filmmakers strove to tell their stories visually, and only poorly made films used many titles. Actors were chosen for their ability to mime and for their facial expressiveness. Their voices were not important.

To make silent films more entertaining, theater owners hired musicians—a single pianist or organist at a small theater, a full orchestra at a large one—to accompany the movies. Audiences seemed content

Despite many career frustrations, Lee de Forest (1873-1961) made his mark as a pioneer both in radio and in motion-picture sound.

with this, using their imaginations to embellish what they saw on the screen. Movie studios were equally satisfied with silent movies. Yet a few innovators envisioned something more: fully synchronized motion-picture sound. Foremost among these was Lee de Forest, an ambitious scientist who knew he could revolutionize the film industry. His invention sparked a race toward sound that would change the movies forever.

Lee de Forest was born in Council Bluffs, Iowa, on August 26, 1873. He was the son of Anna Margaret Robbins and Henry de Forest, a clergyman who believed strongly in education. Lee had an older sister, Mary, and later a younger brother, Charles. Like many fathers, Henry de Forest hoped that his eldest son would follow in his footsteps; he assumed that Lee would become a minister.

In 1879, Lee and his family moved to Alabama, where Henry de Forest took over the presidency of Talladega College, a small African American school that was suffering financial problems. The college grew and prospered under his leadership, but the de Forests were regarded suspiciously by the town's white members, and Lee and his siblings did not make many friends outside the campus community. Shy and not particularly popular, Lee focused his attention on his studies. He was fascinated by science and invention; at age 10, he built a locomotive in his backyard, just to see if he could do it. In 1889, he declared to his father, "I intend to be a machinist and inventor, because I have great talents in that direction."

Lee's determination finally convinced his father that he was bound for a scientific career, not a spiritual one. At the age of 19, Lee left home to attend preparatory school at Mt. Hermon in Massachusetts, and two years later, he entered Yale University's Sheffield Scientific School. His fees were paid by a Yale scholarship fund that had been established by some of his wealthy ancestors. Throughout his three years of college, Lee studied hard and kept inventing. His projects, including a game he tried to sell to Milton Bradley, were unsuccessful. But he continued to believe that it was just a matter of time before he would win fame and fortune.

Tragedy struck the de Forest family in January 1896, when Lee's father suddenly died. Anna de Forest moved east to be near her eldest son, running a boarding house near the Yale campus. After graduating that year, Lee was able to live with his family and continue his work in physics. Concentrating his graduate studies on electrical engineering, he earned his doctorate in 1899.

De Forest moved to Chicago to find a job and worked for a series of companies, including Western Electric. At the same time—in a laboratory in his basement—he was developing his own wireless telegraph system, in which Morse code messages were carried from place to place by radio waves. By 1902, he had started the American De Forest Wireless Telegraph Company and his system was being tested by the United States Navy. The De Forest Wireless Telegraph Tower amazed audiences at the 1904 World's Fair in St. Louis by transmitting messages to

De Forest graduating from Yale in 1899. His dissertation (the paper he wrote to earn his Ph.D.) was entitled "The Reflection of Hertzian Waves at the End of Parallel Wires."

The Audion (above) was a modification of the Fleming valve, a device that converted radio waves into pulses that could be perceived by the human ear. The valve consisted of a glass tube containing a small metal plate and a filament (thin wire). When it was connected to an antenna that received radio waves, an electrical charge flowed from the filament to the plate. De Forest added a metal grid between the two, strengthening this current.

Chicago, 300 miles away (a record distance at the time). On January 15, 1907, de Forest patented his Audion 3-Electrode Amplifier Tube, an invention that amplified, or strengthened, electrical currents—including radio signals. Like many other inventors at the time, he hoped to create a signal strong enough to transmit a human voice.

Soon, however, shady dealings by de Forest's business partners forced his company into bankruptcy. He then formed the De Forest Radio Telephone Company to develop a voice-transmitting system. His invention worked, but again, poor business practices left the company financially shaky. In 1911, de Forest's troubles multiplied when he was charged with a federal crime: using the mail system to perpetrate fraud. He had promoted the Audion tube through the mail, claiming it revolutionized how sound was transmitted—and it did, but authorities did not believe him. De Forest was eventually found not guilty, but the accusation permanently changed his outlook, making him fiercely defensive of his reputation.

As Lee de Forest's business dealings showed, he was a smart man when it came to science and technology, but he was not a good judge of character. This flaw also led to trouble in his personal life. His marriage to Lucille Sheardown began and ended in 1906. Then, on Valentine's Day 1908, Lee married Nora Stanton Blatch. Nora had studied civil engineering and assisted Lee in his lab. He, however, expected his wife to quit working after they were married, an attitude she resented. Their relationship disintegrated by the time their daughter, Harriet, was born in 1909. With his company struggling, Lee moved to Palo Alto, California, to take a job at the Federal Telegraph Company. Nora settled with Harriet in New York, and she and Lee divorced in 1911. In 1912, Lee met and married a singer named Mary Mayo. They would have three children together: Eleanor, born in 1919; Marilyn, in 1924; and Lee Jr., in 1926. Unfortunately, Lee Jr. lived only two days. The tragedy severed the tenuous bond between Lee and Mary, and they also divorced.

In 1913, Western Electric bought the rights to Lee de Forest's Audion for $50,000. He knew this was far less than its value, but he needed the money to support the Radio Telephone Company, which was hanging on by a thread. Later, de Forest discovered that Western Electric's board of directors wanted the Audion so badly that they had been prepared to pay up to half a million dollars for it—10 times what he had gotten. Western Electric's technicians improved the Audion by pumping out the air inside, making it a near-vacuum that could amplify sound up to 130 times without distortion. Although the Audion proved essential to all electronic sound transmission devices, including radio, public address systems, recording, and television, de Forest had already sold his patent and did not share in the profits.

While de Forest struggled with his companies, marriages, and radio technology in general, silent movies had become one of the major sources of entertainment for people around the world. Like many other inventors, de Forest watched the rise of motion pictures with interest. As early as 1913, he began toying with the idea of motion-picture sound, though it was not until 1919 that he seriously turned his thoughts toward the problem. The concept of sound film, however, had been around as long as motion pictures had.

In the early 1890s, Thomas Edison introduced the Kinetophone, which linked his Kinetoscope motion-picture viewing machine to the phonograph he had invented in 1877. Many other inventors also tried to combine picture and sound by using two different machines linked together. But all these systems had the same problem: it was almost impossible to coordinate the two machines so that the sound and picture were precisely synchronized. In addition, amplification was so bad that actors needed to shout their lines during filming and could still barely be heard when the recordings were played back.

The failure of these early systems convinced the motion-picture industry that audiences did not want sound films. "Americans require a restful quiet in the moving picture theater," Edison declared, "and for them talking from the lips of the figures on the screen destroys the illusion. . . . The idea is not practical. The stage is the place for the spoken word." Although experiments with sound continued, by the 1920s, filmmakers, critics, and audiences all believed that silent, black-and-white films were a perfected art form.

The Kinetophone consisted of a Kinetoscope that the viewer watched while wearing headphones that played recorded sound from a cylinder phonograph. Edison could not manage to sell any of these units, as the synchronization was awful and the sound could not be amplified.

THE BREAKTHROUGH

De Forest already had an advantage in motion-picture sound because of his Audion. He also had a new idea: optical sound, in which sound was recorded onto the film itself. He invented a system in which sound waves were converted to electricity and amplified using the Audion. He then converted these electrical signals into light by transmitting them to a bulb that dimmed or brightened depending on the strength of the electrical signal. (A soft sound, represented by a weak electrical signal, would produce a dimmer light than a loud sound). The flickering light from the bulb passed through a narrow slit and was recorded onto film as a thin line along the margin, between the perforations and the images.

When light was shone through the film in the projector, the process was reversed. The light was turned back into electrical signals, which were then converted into sound waves and amplified, reaching the listener's ear through a speaker. The beam of light "played" the sound on film in much the same way that a phonograph needle played records. But in de Forest's system, there was no sound of needles scratching. And because the soundtrack ran along the same strip of film that carried the images, there were fewer problems with synchronizing sound and image.

Since light travels faster than sound, however, there was still a slight time lag between image and soundtrack on de Forest's early films. He soon found that he could solve this problem by recording sound and picture separately on two different negatives and

A piece of de Forest's sound film, showing President Calvin Coolidge giving a speech. The lines along the left side of the film (between the perforations and the picture) are the optical sound recordings.

De Forest's invention was not entirely new; in 1906, Eugene Lauste (1856-1935) had patented a primitive sound-on-film system in England. He ran out of money, however, before he could perfect the concept or interest anyone in buying it.

then printing them together on one positive. This technique also made it possible to add sound to previously made silent films, or to substitute dialogue in another language for films shown abroad. In addition, de Forest developed a way to record multiple soundtracks on one film, allowing music, dialogue, and sound effects to be played simultaneously. Another invention, which he called "noiseless recording," blacked out the soundtrack during periods of no sound, helping to erase stray noise and static.

De Forest filed for a patent on his sound-on-film system, which he dubbed "Phonofilm," in July 1921. After spending a year in Germany perfecting the system, he returned to the United States and founded two companies: the De Forest Phonofilm Corporation, a film production company, and the De Forest Patent Holding Company, which would eventually handle all his sound-recording and sound-projecting devices.

In April 1923, de Forest exhibited his invention in New York City at the Rivoli Theatre. The first Phonofilm starred the singing voice of Eddie Cantor, one of the most popular actors of the era, and dancer Lillian Powell, who performed to the music of Brahms. Audiences were impressed; within a year, 34 theaters were wired for Phonofilm and another 50 were scheduled. De Forest Phonofilm produced more than 1,000 films between 1923 and 1927. They featured speeches from famous people, scenes from plays and operas, instrumentals by top musicians, and popular vaudeville acts. All showed off de Forest's sound system to great effect.

Today I made my first "talking movie" picture—of myself, very hot and somewhat flurried; talked too loud, and the photography was poor, due to white "back drop" and bad placing of the light. But it was at last made, despite all the jinxes and hoodoos—two months behind schedule, and after two years of hard work in preparation—a definite promise of great things to come.
—Lee de Forest in his diary, July 9, 1921

THE RESULT

Phonofilm's success between 1923 and 1926 inspired other companies to research and invest in sound films. The leader was Western Electric. Its Vitaphone system, introduced in 1924, recorded sound not onto film itself, but onto a round, two-inch-thick wax disk. The sounds were amplified so that they caused a needle to vibrate from side to side, cutting grooves in the wax. (A loud sound

In May 1927, the Capitol Theater in New York City advertised de Forest's Phonofilm of famous aviator Charles Lindbergh. It was the first-ever full-length sound newsreel (a short current-events film shown before a feature film).

caused more vibration and made a larger groove than a soft sound.) The wax was treated with chemicals that made copper form on its surface. The copper was then peeled off and used as a negative to produce any number of positive sound disks. These vinyl disks were played on a turntable connected to a film projector. The process was laborious, the wax disks were temperamental (they could only be used in a dust-free environment at a constant temperature, so recording outdoors was difficult), and the copies wore out after about 24 uses and had to be replaced.

The Vitaphone projection machine, with the sound disk visible in the foreground. "When I heard a twelve-piece orchestration on that screen at the Bell Telephone Laboratories [at Western Electric], I could not believe my own ears," recalled an early observer, Harry Warner. "I walked in back of the screen to see if they did not have an orchestra there synchronizing with the picture. They laughed at me. The whole affair was a ten-by-twelve room. There were a lot of bulbs working and things I knew nothing about, but there was not any concealed orchestra."

Despite these disadvantages, the sound quality of Western Electric's system was very good, better even than the early versions of Phonofilm.

Few filmmakers or movie critics noticed, however—or cared. Studios did not want to spend money to build soundproof studios or to rewire movie theaters for sound. They had warehouses full of silent films that they feared would become obsolete if sound films grew popular. But Sam Warner, one of the heads of a minor Hollywood studio called Warner Brothers, was an exception; he was willing to give sound films a chance. In 1925, Warner took a gamble and signed an agreement with Western Electric to produce a series of sound films using the Vitaphone system.

The first Warner Brothers sound film was *Don Juan* in 1926, starring John Barrymore. The film used music and a couple of basic sound effects, but no dialogue. "Who the hell wants to hear actors talk?" said Harry Warner, Sam's brother and president of the studio. "The music—that's the big plus about this." The studio only envisioned Vitaphone as a way of providing music for its films, so that even the smallest theaters could show movies accompanied by the sound of a full orchestra. But it wasn't the music that finally electrified audiences; it was a few improvised lines tossed in by Broadway star Al Jolson in Warner Brothers's 1927 sound musical *The Jazz Singer*. Suddenly, "talkies" were popular. Studios raced to add sound to films already in production. Within about three years, silent movies were nearly obsolete.

In The Jazz Singer, *Al Jolson played an entertainer torn between his Broadway ambitions and the traditions of his Jewish family. His first spoken words in the movie, "Wait a minute! Wait a minute! You ain't heard nothin' yet," are among the most famous lines in film history. In the scene shown here, Jolson performs in blackface, darkening his skin in imitation of the African American minstrel shows that were the source of his songs and style. (Although it is now considered offensive, blackface was common at the time.)*

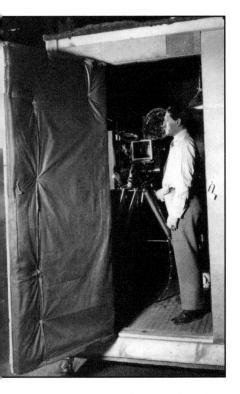

Soundproof camera booths such as this one marred the picture quality (because scenes had to be shot through a plate-glass window) and limited camera movement. Director Cecil B. DeMille supposedly grew so frustrated by this that he brought his camera out of the booth and wrapped blankets around it to muffle the sound, thereby inventing the "blimp"—a soundproof box covering the camera. It was not until the 1960s that manufacturers began to produce quieter cameras.

The rapid switch to sound transformed every aspect of the film industry. Silent films, especially in the early days, had been filmed outdoors using mainly natural light. Sound films, however, had to be shot in enclosed studios, which provided a dust-free and quieter environment than open-air sets. Enclosed studios meant more powerful lights had to be used, which made movie sets as hot as ovens. Makeup changed to look more natural under the unnatural lighting. Cameras, like the sets, had to be soundproofed, encased in booths that kept the noise of whirring gears from being recorded on film.

Suddenly faced with a need for screenwriters who could produce detailed scripts and quality dialogue, movie studios imported Broadway playwrights to write the stories for sound films. Actors had to change, too. Their ability to mime was no longer important; they now must have pleasant voices and speak proper English. Although many silent stars made the transition to sound successfully, others faded, replaced by a wave of stage actors from New York. By making movie musicals possible, sound also opened up new opportunities for singers and dancers. At the same time, however, thousands of musicians who had worked as accompanists in movie theaters were no longer needed. Theaters themselves faced difficulties; about 5,000 movie houses were forced to close because they could not afford to install the new sound equipment. (Business did boom in remaining theaters, as record numbers of people attended films in 1929 and 1930.)

Silent film had served to unite audiences in many countries, but sound actually divided the international film community. Silent films reached a worldwide audience simply by translating the title cards into other languages, but recording new dialogue for sound films was laborious and costly. The largest film audiences were in the United States, so many foreign actors and directors were forced to work in English or else make films in their native languages, which limited their financial success.

All the seemingly small adjustments required for sound films added up to a revolution in the motion-picture industry, and even in how audiences viewed film. (Talking during films, for example, was now considered rude and socially unacceptable.) For all the changes sound required, it is remarkable that the conversion took only a few years. Unfortunately for Lee de Forest, the rush had not been for his Phonofilm, but for Western Electric's Vitaphone.

De Forest's film company, despite having an early advantage in the race to sound, had focused its production on short arts or current events pieces to be shown before feature films, rather than on feature films themselves. De Forest wanted nothing to do with cheap, popular movies, envisioning sound film as a separate form of entertainment that would allow wider audiences to experience live events, much as radio did. But films of speeches, lectures, and Broadway plays were not enough to keep his business in the black. In 1928, while the conversion to sound film was in full swing in Hollywood, de Forest sold his ruined company.

In 1930, de Forest remarried, to actor Marie Mosquini. This fourth union was apparently a happy one, but de Forest's business life remained troublesome. His lawsuits were legendary. He fought a 20-year legal battle with Edwin Armstrong over rights to the regenerative circuit, which strengthened radio transmissions. Armstrong patented the device in 1913, basing his work on de Forest's Audion design; de Forest then patented a similar circuit that he called the "ultra Audion" in 1914. The case finally ended in 1934, when the U.S. Supreme Court ruled in de Forest's favor. (Despite the legal victory, however, most historians credit Armstrong for the invention.) Another scientist, Theodore Case, also sued de Forest. De Forest had, by agreement, used Case's patented invention, a photoelectric cell called the Aeo light that produced the varying light intensities de Forest needed to record sound onto film. Case withdrew his permission in late 1925, developed his own sound-on-film system (Fox Movietone), and sued de Forest for continuing to use the device. The protracted legal wrangling hurt de Forest's business and his reputation.

While his Phonofilm Corporation failed, de Forest's inventions had spurred other scientists to greater heights in sound technology. Eventually, Hollywood forsook Vitaphone and turned to optical sound—the very system that de Forest had pioneered. In 1960, the Academy of Motion Picture Arts and Sciences (AMPAS) gave Lee de Forest an Honorary Academy Award for his contribution to motion-picture sound.

Lee de Forest's Academy Award

Despite his troubled career and his unwise business decisions, de Forest had a long life as an electronics engineer and inventor. He received his last patent in 1957, when he was 84, for an automatic telephone-dialing device. By the time of his death in Los Angeles on June 30, 1961, he had received more than 180 patents. Though material wealth proved fleeting for Lee de Forest, he is remembered as one of the great scientists of the twentieth century, as well one of the great contributors to the technology of motion pictures.

De Forest directs a cameraman in using his Phonofilm equipment.

CHAPTER FOUR

Herbert Kalmus and Technicolor

"Up to now, the moving picture industry has been like an artist who was allowed only to use pencil or charcoal," said director Rouben Mamoulian in 1935. Since their invention more than 40 years before, motion pictures had existed only in black and white. Filmmakers had mastered the art of using expressive shadows and dramatic contrasts between light and dark, but without color, they could not equal the full intensity of human vision. When vivid reds, bright blues, and brilliant greens finally appeared onscreen, it was a revelation for audiences and filmmakers alike. "Now Technicolor has given us paints," Mamoulian declared of the company that created the first successful method for making color motion pictures. Thanks to Herbert Kalmus, founder and leader of Technicolor, the film industry gained a new tool for reproducing reality and creating worlds of fantasy— in every color of the rainbow.

Herbert Kalmus (1881-1963) founded the company and invented the process that became synonymous with color motion pictures— Technicolor.

Herbert Thomas Kalmus was born to Benjamin and Ada Kalmus on November 9, 1881, in Chelsea, Massachusetts. His family soon moved to South Boston, where he grew up enjoying his two favorite interests, baseball and piano. When Herbert was eight years old, his mother died suddenly of acute appendicitis. His father remarried, but three years later he died of Bright's disease, an inflammation of the kidneys. Herbert was given the choice of living with his uncle and grandmother or with his stepmother's family. He opted for the latter, where there would be children his age in the household.

When Herbert was 16, his guardian informed him it was time to get a job. He soon found work as an office boy and eventually a bookkeeper. This, plus a piano-playing job at the YMCA, allowed him to save up enough money to go to college at age 18. Herbert was admitted to the Massachusetts Institute of Technology (MIT), or as it was known then, Boston Tech. After trying and then becoming bored with mining engineering and chemistry, the young man was finally satisfied with physics. He enjoyed his college life immensely, and in his senior year he made a fateful decision to marry a fiery sales clerk and model, Natalie Dunphy.

After graduation in 1904, Herbert and his best friend, Daniel Comstock, both won fellowships that funded graduate studies in Europe. While Herbert and Dan studied or bicycled around the countryside, Natalie absorbed the art museums of Germany and Switzerland. Realizing that her husband was wrapped up in his studies, Natalie eventually went

When Herbert Kalmus became a physics major at Boston Tech, Dan Comstock was the only other student in the department. At that time, just two other people had ever graduated from the physics program.

home. Herbert and Dan returned to the U.S. after earning their Ph.D. degrees in 1906, and they taught for a few years at Boston Tech and other schools.

In 1912, the two friends—plus a mechanical genius named William Burton Wescott—formed a scientific consulting company in Boston called Kalmus, Comstock, & Wescott. William Coolidge, a lawyer with money to invest in new projects, approached Kalmus and his partners about a motion-picture device called the Vanoscope. Motion-picture technology was barely two decades old at the time, and films were so dim and choppy that they were often called "flickers." The Vanoscope was intended to make films appear smoother, to "take the flickers out of flickers." Coolidge wanted Kalmus to tell him if the invention was a good investment. After some investigation, Kalmus reported that it was too impractical for widespread use, but the idea had piqued his interest in film technology. He suggested something else for Coolidge to invest in: color motion pictures.

Although attempts had already been made to bring color to motion pictures, the cost was too high and the quality too low to be useful. Early methods involved hand-coloring the film after it was shot. A later technique, the most advanced so far, was the British Kinemacolor Process, introduced in 1909. Kinemacolor produced a color image by shooting the same picture twice, once through a green filter and once through a red one. One film negative recorded the green light in a scene, since that was all the green filter would let through, and another

Kalmus invented many useful processes at Kalmus, Comstock, & Wescott, including one that eventually made lie detectors and electrocardiograms possible. He also developed a way to destroy bacteria by electrical radiation, as well as a Photo-Speed Recorder to identify traffic law violators. Although his inventions were sound, the technology was too complicated to interest investors.

filter: a colored screen that controls the amount and type of light that passes through it; a green filter, for instance, blocks out all colors of light except green

recorded the red. The two strips of film were in black and white, but projecting them together—one through a red filter and the other through a green one—made the separate images appear to merge and created a limited range of colors. Kinemacolor was known as an "additive color" system since the red and green hues were added by filters during projection, combining to produce other colors.

Kinemacolor was innovative, but it had its problems. The special camera used a rotating wheel to alternate rapidly between red and green filters after each frame. Thus, the red and green images were not photographed at exactly the same time, and they differed slightly. When the films were shown in the Kinemacolor projector, viewers could often see color "fringes" where the two sets of pictures did not match up—for instance, a horse might appear to have two tails, one red and one green.

Kalmus, Comstock, and Wescott knew they could improve on Kinemacolor, but they would need a substantial amount of money to pay for experiments and tests. Coolidge advanced them $10,000 and helped them organize the Technicolor Motion Picture Corporation, which Kalmus named after his and Comstock's alma mater, Boston Tech. Kalmus served as president and general manager; the company's first laboratory was a railroad car. Although there were many technical challenges to overcome, Kalmus had absolute faith in his team of technicians, telling them, "if you can't do it, it can't be done." By 1917, the company had perfected "Technicolor Process #1" to the point where it could produce a short color movie.

"TECHNICOLOR"—a beautiful name, a meaningful word, easy to remember, hard to forget, and possessing a full measure of significance for a company aiming to revolutionize the motion-picture world.
—Herbert Kalmus

Process #1 was still an additive color system, but it corrected many of Kinemacolor's faults. Light entered through the camera lens and hit a small prism, a piece of glass that split the single beam of light into two identical beams. One beam passed through a red filter and struck a negative, recording the red light in the scene; the other beam passed through a green filter to a different negative, recording the green light. When these two films were developed, they appeared black and white. A special projector then shone a beam of light through each of the films at the same time. Each beam again passed through a red or green filter, and another prism combined them into a single beam that left the projector and brought the color images to the screen. Although this method could not project a wider range of color than Kinemacolor did, it looked more natural. Because both sets of film were shot simultaneously, Technicolor movies were much clearer and easier to watch.

Technicolor made its own amateurish film using the new process, *The Gulf Between* (1917). Viewers and critics marveled at the color, but, as Kalmus admitted, the film "did not have the dramatic power or star performances to pull audiences into the theater." In addition, the Technicolor process was not appealing to movie-theater owners because it required the extra costs of a special projector and a highly trained projectionist. Hollywood, too, remained reluctant to adopt Technicolor. Movie studios believed color films hurt viewers' eyes, distracted from a film's story, cost too much, and required too many adjustments to lighting, makeup, sets, and actors.

One of Technicolor's earliest color cameras, from about 1916

The new process throws upon the screen a continual succession of pictures in natural colors that copies nature with the fidelity of a finely executed oil painting. Many of the landscapes and water scenes are . . . remarkable.
—a review of *The Gulf Between*

THE BREAKTHROUGH

Herbert Kalmus was already pushing his crew to develop a better color system, and the result was Technicolor Process #2. In this process, the image again was split by prisms and passed through filters. This time, the separate green and red components of the scene were recorded on the same negative, one just above the other. Two positive prints were made, one from the red images and one from the green. Each positive, however, was only half the thickness of a normal strip of film. The two positives were then cemented together, back to back, and put through a special developing process that added red dye to the side of the film containing the red images and green dye to the other side. The result was a single strip of colored film with only one frame for each image. When a beam of light was shone through it, it showed a two-color representation of the original scene. The images were clearer than in Process #1, and theaters could show the films without buying new projectors or retraining their projectionists.

In 1922, Technicolor hired professional actors and a director to shoot *The Toll of the Sea* using Process #2. This film brought Technicolor's first profit since the company's founding. But there were still problems. Since it was made of two strips layered together, Technicolor film was slightly thicker than a typical strip of black-and-white film, causing it to warp in the projector. And the process was still not practical enough to be widely used in Hollywood. Technicolor film was far more expensive to produce than black-and-white film, and it could not be developed fast enough. (Filmmakers needed to watch "rushes"—early, unedited prints—soon after footage had been shot, so that they could see how the scenes had turned out.)

But Kalmus was already working on improvements. In 1926, he introduced Technicolor Process #3, which eliminated the need to cement two separate strips of film together. The dye from each frame of one of the colored films was printed onto a special clear film, called the base, by sandwiching the dyed and base films together under high pressure and then separating them. This was repeated with the other colored film and the same base film (which by then had some dye on it already). As the two layers of dye combined, they created colors on the base, which could be shown by a normal projector without the warping problems of Process #2. This process is called dye transfer printing.

The Viking in 1928 was the first feature film to use Process #3. Not only was warping no longer a problem, but the images were much clearer and the colors were richer. Based on the quality of this film, Warner Brothers agreed to produce a series of 20 feature-length color films using Process #3. Other studios also began work on color projects, and by 1930, Technicolor held contracts for 36 feature-length films. Process #3 still had one major problem, however: using only two dyes meant that it was impossible to capture the real world's full range of colors on film. Something more was needed.

Producing Technicolor film with Process #2 cost the company between 15 and 25 cents per foot. In contrast, black-and-white film cost about 3 1/2 cents per foot.

A Technicolor Process #3 camera from around 1926

Technicolor designed this 1930 advertisement to interest consumers in its technology and convince them that its color films looked "natural."

By 1932, Kalmus had that "something more": the three-color Technicolor process. Called Process #4 but often referred to as "Glorious Technicolor" in the marketing slogans, it used red, blue, and green to accurately reproduce the full spectrum of colors. With prisms and filters, a special camera captured the image simultaneously on three separate negatives (one for each color). These were then developed, dyed, and combined into one film using the dye transfer technique.

Pictures shot in Process #4 were clearer and more vivid than anything seen on the big screen before. Use of the process was pioneered by Walt Disney, who contracted to use Technicolor in his animated films. The color cartoons were so popular they played for weeks or even months, and soon Hollywood studios were clamoring for Technicolor. In 1935, *Becky Sharp* became the first feature-length, live-action film shot in Process #4. Over the next few years, more and more filmmakers realized the appeal and value of using color.

To encourage studios to change to color, Herbert Kalmus offered a color advisory service—a

The first movie made with Technicolor Process #4 was the cartoon short *Flowers and Trees* (1932), for which Walt Disney won his first Academy Award.

Director (and later actor) Henry Fonda used the Technicolor three-color camera to shoot The Trail of the Lonesone Pine *in 1936.*

Natalie Kalmus in her office at Technicolor. As she described her job, "We carefully analyze each sequence and scene to ascertain what dominant mood or emotion is to be expressed . . . [and] plan to use the appropriate color or set of colors which will suggest that mood. . . . We then prepare a color chart, using actual samples of fabrics and materials, for the entire production."

support group of designers and camera operators that was leased to studios along with the Technicolor equipment. This operation was managed by Natalie Kalmus. She had always assisted with Herbert's experiments in color, coordinating sets and costumes for *The Gulf Between* and other films. Their marriage was tumultuous, however; Herbert was absorbed in his work, and Natalie often had outbursts of temper, intense jealousy, and illness. In 1921, the couple had divorced, but Natalie continued her involvement in Technicolor. Although their rocky working relationship took a toll on Herbert

Kalmus's personal life, Natalie was adept at her work as a color consultant. Under her supervision, directors were taught how to "think in color." Filming techniques, lighting, makeup, sets, props, and costumes were all closely analyzed for their suitability for color filming. Her name appeared in the credits of hundreds of Technicolor movies, becoming more closely connected in the public's mind with the innovative color process than Herbert Kalmus was.

One of the most dramatic and memorable examples of the three-color process was the phenomenally successful *The Wizard of Oz*, released in 1939. The film used the change from black and white to color to establish the contrast between Dorothy's everyday life in Kansas and the fantasy land of Oz. The opening scenes in Kansas were shot in sepia (black-and-white film washed in a brown bath). The transition to color occurred in hand-tinted frames, as Dorothy first saw the colorful land of Oz through the door of her black-and-white farmhouse. Dorothy's adventures in Oz were filmed in Technicolor, and at the end, she returned home to colorless Kansas.

That same year, Hollywood released the long-awaited Civil War epic *Gone with the Wind*, possibly the best use of Technicolor on film. The technology helped to make *Gone with the Wind* a big winner at the Academy Awards that year, with 10 awards including Best Picture. Kalmus also took home an Academy Award, for Technicolor's contribution "in successfully bringing three-color feature production to the screen."

The three separate negatives in the Technicolor Process #4 camera

Gone with the Wind cost an unprecedented $4 million and took three years to make. Technicolor shot 449,512 feet (88 hours) of film for the project, of which 20,300 feet (3 hours and 45 minutes) were used in the finished movie.

The filming of the Munchkinland sequence, the first color scene of The Wizard of Oz. *The movie's 25-acre set featured 122 buildings, painted in more than 60 different colors.*

THE RESULT

The gradual shift to color changed the entire movie industry. Color film required much stronger lighting, since the light entering the camera was dimmed by the prisms and filters it had to pass through. Casts and crews suffered under hot, bright lights until 1939, when Technicolor introduced high-speed film that could absorb light more quickly, cutting lighting needs almost in half. Makeup changed, as well. In black-and-white films, actors had worn thick, heavy makeup that made their skin appear flawless and overemphasized their eyes and lips. In color, however, makeup needed to be more subdued, realistically matching skin tones. Costumes and sets faced similar adjustments. Some actors were deathly afraid of how they would look onscreen in color, but many others thrived on the way it showed off their glamour. Technicolor helped develop a whole new theory of taste and beauty in film.

By the 1950s, color filming was widely available through various companies, so Technicolor lost some of its competitive edge. In 1954, the bulky three-strip Technicolor camera was used for the last time in American films. With Monopack, a process jointly developed by Technicolor and Eastman Kodak, images could now be recorded on a single strip of black-and-white film, which was coated in layers of emulsions that were each sensitive to a different type of light (red, green, and blue). These layers were made into three separate negatives and then developed using the dye transfer method. Eventually, the process that had made Technicolor a household name became obsolete when Eastman Kodak introduced Eastmancolor, the first true color film. The company continued to prosper, however, by changing its focus from movie production to color film processing.

Herbert Kalmus retired from Technicolor in 1960 at the age of 78, and he died on July 11, 1963. The company he founded won, between 1939 and 1995, nine Scientific and Technical Academy Awards. Although color movies made with other processes faded over time, the brilliant hues of the Technicolor three-color method did not deteriorate. Even though his famous process is no longer used, Herbert Kalmus's legacy remains true, in glorious Technicolor.

Betty Grable, Rita Hayworth, and Carmen Miranda were among the stars who became known for their beauty in Technicolor. *Life* magazine called Lucille Ball "Technicolor Tessie" because of her bright red hair and blue eyes. Maureen O'Hara was dubbed "The Queen of Technicolor," since she appeared in the footage Technicolor used to woo the studios. In appreciation for this publicity, the company sent her roses in every color of the rainbow every time she began a new film.

Although almost every color movie made between 1925 and 1950 used Technicolor, these were only 12 percent of the total number of Hollywood films made during that time. Even into the 1960s, at least half of all movies were still shot in black and white. Hollywood did not convert entirely to color until the advent of color television made it a competitive necessity. By 1970, 94 percent of American feature films were made in color, and today it costs more to film in black and white than it does to use color.

CHAPTER FIVE

Linwood Dunn and the Optical Printer

"How did they do that?" is perhaps the most common question heard in movie theaters today. Special effects can be so spectacular that they are the main attraction in some blockbuster films. Even classics, like Orson Welles's 1941 *Citizen Kane* or the earliest *Star Trek* television shows and films, still make people wonder what magic was concocted behind the scenes. For many decades, the answer to "How did they do that?" was "Linwood Dunn."

Linwood Gale Dunn was born in Brooklyn, New York, on December 27, 1904. While growing up he trained himself as a musician, and he performed in a dance band while attending Manual Training High School. After graduation, he got a summer job at a music publisher called Hamilton S. Gordon. His music connection helped him afford a new alto saxophone, so he could play in better bands. Dunn's real interest, however, was a newly popular form of entertainment—motion pictures. In 1923,

By developing a device that allowed filmmakers to combine separately filmed scenes in many different ways, Linwood Dunn (1904-1998) revolutionized motion-picture visual effects.

he landed his first job in the motion-picture industry when he was hired as a projectionist for the American Motion Picture Corporation of New York City. In this position, he ran the projector for churches, schools, and other groups that rented films. But when the company went out of business, he went back to playing in bands.

Dunn's uncle, Spencer Gordon Bennet, was a stuntman and actor who had recently turned to directing. In 1925, Bennet gave Dunn a job as an assistant cameraman at the Pathé film production company. Dunn had just accepted a job playing in a jazz band at a summer resort, and, he later remembered, "I had to quit in a hurry, as there would be two others waiting to take my place if I didn't show up [at the Pathé job] on time." At Pathé, Dunn was put to work on Bennet's second directorial effort, a serial called *The Green Archer*. (Serial films carried a single plot through multiple parts, which were shown weekly in theaters.)

In 1926, Pathé moved its serial unit from New York to Hollywood, California. Dunn decided to go along. He continued as assistant cameraman on four more serials, and in 1927 he earned a new responsibility, as second cameraman for *Hawk of the Hills*. Dunn photographed the negatives that would be used to create foreign versions of the film. He also began to learn how to use visual effects.

When Dunn was beginning his career, the film industry was still very young. The first motion pictures had been created just a decade before he was born. The technology to create color or sound films

Frenchman Charles Pathé (1863-1957) founded Societé Pathé Frères with his three brothers—Emile, Théophile, and Jacques—in 1896 to manufacture cameras and projectors. The company soon began producing films, and by 1912, it was one of the largest moviemaking organizations in the world. Among its innovations were a hand-colored film process, Pathécolor, and the introduction of newsreels (short films of current events that were shown in theaters before feature films).

had not yet been developed, but filmmakers had begun experimenting with visual effects immediately. Visual effects (also known as special effects) are "tricks" that create the illusion of something that did not really happen during the actual filming. Often, they are used to create fantastic scenes of the impossible, such as a man flying or a dinosaur destroying a city. But visual effects can also save

Linwood Dunn (right) assists his uncle (center, with megaphone) in filming a scene near Catalina, California, for a Pathé serial.

time and money by creating scenes of reality, such as a large city or a speeding car. To modern audiences, early visual effects may seem unsophisticated. In the days when motion pictures were new, however, people were so unaccustomed to watching films that some would cover their heads when they saw rainfall on the screen.

Viewers of the 1895 short film *The Execution of Mary, Queen of Scots* witnessed the first known visual effect, a simple technique called a substitution shot. Director Alfred Clark devised a way to show the queen's head being severed without harming an actor. In the scene where the queen was to be killed, filming stopped just before the executioner dropped his axe. The actor playing the queen was replaced with a dummy and filming resumed. When the axe fell, it decapitated the dummy.

That same year, a French magician and theater owner named George Méliès was captivated by the first public screening of the Lumière brothers' Cinematographe. Realizing he could create a whole new form of magic through motion pictures, he launched his own company, Star Films. Among his earliest visual effects was a technique called multiple exposure. By photographing more than one image onto the same piece of film, Méliès could make people and objects disappear and reappear or change into other forms; for example, a woman seemed to transform into a skeleton in his film *The Vanishing Lady* (1896). Using the principle of the substitution shot, Méliès also developed an effect called stop-motion animation, in which a miniature figure was photographed one frame at a time as it was moved in extremely small increments. When the film was run at regular speed, it created the illusion that the object was moving. Méliès's best-known work, the science-fiction film *Le Voyage Dans La Lune (A Trip to the Moon)* (1902), employed a number of his newly developed visual effects: for example, the Moon was portrayed as a live human face.

Méliès's "trick films" were so popular that other filmmakers began devising their own visual effects to attract audiences. In 1903, Edwin S. Porter's *The Great Train Robbery* featured the first matte shot, in which one part of the camera lens was covered with a matte, or mask, during filming to prevent that area of the film from being exposed to light and capturing an image. The film was then rewound and reshot—this time with a matte over the other part of the camera lens—to add a second image in the part of the film that had not yet been exposed. This technique allowed Porter to show a locomotive rushing past outside the window of a "train station" (actually the studio).

Four years later, director Norman O. Dawn pioneered the glass shot. He discovered that he could alter or extend real scenery on film through the use of highly detailed paintings on sheets of glass placed between the camera and the actors. The camera would film through the clear parts of the glass, but the painted parts would appear to be part of the scene. (This technique was often used to add height to studio sets, which were only one or two stories tall.) Dawn later developed a way of combining

Méliès discovered the magic of visual effects by pure accident when his camera jammed while he was filming a street scene. "It took a minute to release the film and get the camera going again," he later recalled. "During this minute the people, buses, vehicles, had of course moved. Projecting the film, having joined the break, I suddenly saw an omnibus changed into a hearse and men into women. The trick of substitution, [also] called the trick of stop-action, was discovered."

A glass shot created by Norman O. Dawn in 1908. The balcony where the actors stood was real, but the rest of the scene was painted on a sheet of glass.

filmed scenery with paintings by using a matte shot: first the real scene was filmed with the unwanted portions blacked out, and then the paintings (known as matte paintings) were filmed in the unexposed part of the film. Dawn's innovations helped filmmakers re-create exotic locations without having to move the entire team of actors, technicians, and equipment out of the studio.

Visual-effects techniques continued to evolve through the next decade, and by the 1920s they were virtually a requirement in most successful movies. Major film studios established departments solely to handle the demand for such effects. It was during this period of innovation and development that Linwood Dunn began his career in motion pictures.

Dunn worked on 13 serial films before he became first cameraman for the 1929 film *Queen of the Northwoods*. But shortly after filming ended, the Pathé company encountered financial difficulties—just as many other companies did during the Great Depression. As Pathé verged on bankruptcy, it reduced its shooting schedule. Dunn supplemented his diminishing income by performing in jazz clubs.

That year, Dunn was offered a temporary job as an assistant at a new film studio called RKO Radio Pictures. The job was supposed to last only two days, but Linwood Dunn ended up staying with RKO for 28 years. Almost immediately, he began experimenting with several new visual effects. One of his earliest contributions was a homemade zoom lens, which could gradually change focus ("zoom in") to make it appear that the camera was moving closer to the thing it was filming. He also became skilled in a technique known as back projection, in which a scene was projected onto a screen behind the actors so that it appeared they were actually in the location being shown. For example, the actors could sit in a car seat in the studio while, behind them, the background scene made it appear as though they were driving through the streets of San Francisco.

Dunn also began to investigate a new way to make transitions, visual effects used to shift from one scene to another. One common transition was the wipe, which made it appear that a shot was being pushed off the screen by another shot. Another was the fade, in which the screen gradually changed from black to image (fade in) or from image to black (fade out). A dissolve was a more complex version of the fade, allowing a scene to be gradually replaced by another; one image faded out as the next faded in. At the time, all these effects were produced "in the camera," or manually—a camera operator would slowly cover the lens with an opaque sheet of paper. Dunn decided there had to be a better, less clumsy way.

THE BREAKTHROUGH

Dunn experimented with automating visual effects using a process called optical printing. "Optical printing, or 'projection printing,' as it is sometimes called, is a process of rephotographing [images] . . . from one motion-picture film to another," Dunn explained. The process was used to create copies of original motion-picture footage. Filmmakers had used various makeshift optical printing devices since the industry's earliest days, and by Dunn's time, each studio had its own unique, handmade optical printer. These machines combined a standard motion-picture camera containing unexposed (blank) film with a projector containing exposed film (on which a movie had been shot). The projector, precisely synchronized with the camera, cast images directly onto the unexposed film to create a copy.

Dunn realized that with some modifications, film technicians could use an optical printer to create better visual effects. He added controls to his equipment so that he could create fades, dissolves, and wipes during the printing process instead of during filming. For instance, a wipe between two shots could be created by fitting the optical printer's camera with a "blade" that moved mechanically across the first image, progressively covering it and leaving more and more of the frame unexposed. Then the film could be rewound and the second shot printed onto the unexposed parts of the frame as the blade moved in reverse across it. Similarly, Dunn could create matte shots by masking off part of a frame of

To create a fadeout at the end of a scene, Dunn printed the scene while gradually closing the camera's shutter a little more after each frame, reducing the amount of light that reached the copied film. Making a dissolve from one scene to another involved the same technique. After the fadeout from the first scene, the film was rewound and the projector was loaded with the second scene. Another exposure was made, this time with the camera's shutter gradually opening— so that the second scene faded in as the first one faded out.

film as it was printed and then printing a section of a different film onto the masked area. He could also use the optical printer to change the film speed: by skipping every other frame, he could speed up the action, while if he wanted to create the illusion of slow motion, he exposed the same frame twice. He could even turn shots into closeups by moving the printer's camera closer to the projector.

The first film featuring Dunn's homemade visual-effects optical printer was *Ringside* (1929). He

Linwood Dunn (left) with a colleague and Dunn's visual-effects optical printer

soon realized, however, that optical printing was useful not only for reproducing effects previously made by hand, but also for devising new effects that could not have been achieved manually. Among them were a wide variety of wipe effects: with a curtain wipe, for instance, a new scene was revealed as the old one slid upward, while in the turnover wipe, an image appeared to flip over to reveal another. The new wipes gave directors more of a choice about how to move from one scene to another. These transitions between scenes were important; if badly done, they were distracting at best and confusing at worst. But smooth transitions could enhance the audience's enjoyment and understanding of the story.

Dunn and his colleagues scattered the new effects throughout a short film entitled *This Is Harris* (1933). "These wipes met with such entire approval," Dunn later wrote, "that they were called for again in *Melody Cruise* [1933]. *Flying Down to Rio* [1933] was the third RKO picture to require a large assortment of these effects. In all cases we were given a very free hand in the selection of the type of effect to be used." Dunn was appointed head of RKO's Optical Effect Department and later became head of the Camera Effects Department. Known as the "king" of optical printing, he created visual effects for nearly all of RKO's feature films over a span of decades, including *King Kong* (1933), *The Last Days of Pompeii* (1935), *The Hunchback of Notre Dame* (1939), *Citizen Kane* (1941), *It's a Wonderful Life* (1946), *The Thing* (1951), and many Fred Astaire and Ginger Rogers musicals. "At RKO

I used the optical printer, a little or a lot, on almost every picture," Dunn recalled.

Citizen Kane is one of the most famous examples in film history of the use of visual effects. "I think . . . that for Citizen Kane I did some of my most involved effects work of my career," Dunn remembered. He estimated that director Orson Welles ordered as much as 50 percent of the movie's footage to be optically improved or altered in some way. Dunn used his optical printer to create effects

The climactic scene of the musical Flying Down to Rio *featured dancers on the wings of airplanes that appeared to be flying high in the air. In reality, the planes were suspended from the roof of a hangar, and wind machines were used to simulate motion. Dunn's optical printer then combined this footage with images of clouds.*

> Welles didn't know at first what an optical printer was. When he was finally introduced to it and learned that there was a tool that could alter scenes after they were shot, then he used it like a paint brush. Boy, he'd come in and want work done that I would say was impossible—but he'd persevere.
> —Linwood Dunn

such as a scene in which the camera appeared to zoom through a skylight into a nightclub during a storm. Welles started with the camera outside the skylight, zoomed in, and stopped right at the glass, then resumed filming inside the skylight and continued the zoom. During printing, Dunn combined the two shots. To smooth out the transition between them, he created what appeared to be lightning flashes on the skylight by overexposing some of the frames, making them brighter.

Despite their usefulness and popularity, optical printers were not produced commercially. They were still largely makeshift devices assembled by individual studios and filmmakers. Then, in 1942, the Eastman Kodak Company asked Dunn to assist in developing an optical printer for the U.S. Armed Forces Photographic Units. The U.S. government commissioned Dunn and a longtime associate, Cecil Love, to design the device. The Acme Tool and Manufacturing Company in Burbank, California, built the equipment to Dunn and Love's specifications, and in 1944 the world's first manufactured, publicly available visual-effects optical printer was born. That year, Dunn and Love accepted an Academy Award in Technical Achievement for their device, the Acme-Dunn Optical Printer.

THE RESULT

Linwood Dunn continued to develop innovative visual-effects techniques throughout his career at RKO. When the studio went out of business in 1957, Dunn arranged to lease its special-effects laboratories and merged them with Film Effects of Hollywood, a company he had founded in 1946. Film Effects manufactured the Acme-Dunn Optical Printer for sale to commercial studios and special-effects labs, and Dunn offered technical consulting to customers who purchased the equipment.

Dunn also added a new capability to his optical printer: blue-screening. Using this technique

Linwood Dunn (left) and his associate, Cecil Love, work on a visual effect for the opening credits of the musical West Side Story *(1961) at Film Effects of Hollywood.*

Film Effects of Hollywood created visual effects for classic movies such as It's a Mad, Mad, Mad, Mad World *(1963),* My Fair Lady *(1964), and* The Great Race *(1965), as well as for television programs such as* Star Trek *and* Wonder Woman.

required a subject to be filmed in front of a bright blue (or sometimes orange or green) screen. The vividly colored background was easier to see and to remove during optical printing, when it was replaced with a separately filmed background scene. One effect that could result was that an actor or object appeared to be flying or floating. Blue-screen photography was used in many films, including Cecil B. DeMille's 1956 epic *The Ten Commandments* (when Charlton Heston's character, Moses, parted the Red Sea), Disney's 1964 film *Mary Poppins* (when the title character floated up through the air with her open umbrella), and the 1982 blockbuster *E. T.: The Extra-Terrestrial* (when Elliott and his alien friend rode off into the sky on a bicycle).

A highly respected figure in the motion-picture industry, Linwood Dunn served two terms as president of the American Society of Cinematographers. He was a member of the Society of Motion Picture and Television Engineers and the Society of Photographic Scientists and Engineers. He also wrote many articles and delivered numerous lectures on visual-effects cinematography. In 1967, Dunn was nominated for a Special Visual Effects Academy Award for his work on the film *Hawaii*. In 1980, Dunn and Cecil Love's 1944 award was "upgraded" to an Academy Award of Merit for the design and construction of the Acme-Dunn Optical Printer. Dunn also received two special Academy Awards: a Medal of Commendation in 1978, and the prestigious Gordon E. Sawyer Award, the Academy's top honor for technical achievement, in 1984.

In 1997, 92-year-old Linwood Dunn was still striving to apply the newest technology to filmmaking. He was perfecting a process that he called "Electronic Cinema." Instead of making thousands of prints of their films, motion-picture studios could use Electronic Cinema to distribute them to theaters in digital format through fiber-optic lines. Since each print of a film cost about $2,000, the process could save motion-picture studios millions of dollars. It would also help prevent piracy (stealing of copyrighted material) because the information could be encrypted, or put into code, for digital transmission.

fiber-optics: bundles of thin glass fibers through which light (and images) can travel

Linwood Dunn died on May 20, 1998, at age 93. His optical printer was the standard for creating visual effects for 50 years, until the mid-1990s, when computerized, digital effects became possible. Still, Dunn's invention remained one of the film industry's most valuable tools for creating the dazzling visual effects that twenty-first-century moviegoers are accustomed to seeing.

Those who knew Linwood Dunn described him as an amiable man who was eager to share what he learned with younger filmmakers and technicians. Robert Abel, one of the earliest members of the Visual Effects Society, fondly remembered discussing techniques with Dunn over lunch at Dunn's favorite restaurant—a Sizzler Steak House in Hollywood. "He believed he was endowed with a special power or magic and felt that his . . . purpose was to pass this on," said Abel. "The tools got better, but nobody ever got better than him."

CHAPTER SIX

Mike Todd
and Todd-AO

After World War II ended in 1945, the film industry faced its most serious threat: television. In 1947, there were only 44,000 television sets in the United States, compared to 40 million radios. Ten years later, 41 million American homes had televisions, and people were staying home instead of going to the movies. Between 1948 and 1952, the number of movie tickets sold per week in the United States dropped by half. Hollywood fought back by emphasizing the differences between television and what came to be called "the moviegoing experience."

To attract audiences, studios tried three-dimensional (3-D) films that made pictures appear to jump off the screen. They developed stereophonic sound, which used multiple soundtracks to re-create sound realistically in different locations around the audience. And they began making movie screens even bigger. Several new widescreen systems were introduced in the 1950s, becoming the era's most lasting

Producer Mike Todd (1909-1958) poses with his son, Mike Todd Jr. (1929-2002), while promoting Around the World in 80 Days *in 1956. The film was a sensation thanks to Todd's innovative widescreen system, Todd-AO.*

contribution to motion pictures. The huge pictures surrounded audiences and made them feel as though they were part of the action. Widescreen films were shown in special theaters, only two or three times a day, with presold, higher-priced tickets and reserved seating. They were presented as unique attractions, more similar to live theater than to ordinary movies or television. It is not surprising, therefore, that the innovator best suited to developing and promoting such a spectacular format was a bombastic Broadway show producer named Mike Todd.

Mike Todd was born Avrom Hirsch Goldbogen in Minneapolis, Minnesota, on June 22, 1909. He was the second-youngest of nine children of Chaim Goldbogen and Sophia Hellerman, Jewish immigrants from Poland. Avrom was their first child born in the United States. He was soon nicknamed "Toat" by his older siblings, due to his youthful inability to pronounce the word "coat."

School did not interest Avrom. The only time it caught his attention was when his school mounted a production of *The Mikado*, a musical by W. S. Gilbert and Arthur Sullivan. Avrom was stage manager of the show, and it was a hit. But after the Goldbogens moved from Minneapolis to Chicago in 1918, the distractions of the big city made education seem even less appealing to Avrom. Eager to make money, he quit high school during his first year and worked at a series of different jobs—including pharmacist, shoe salesman, and store-window decorator. On Valentine's Day 1927, at the age of 17, he married Bertha Freshman.

Once he built an immense toothpaste tube that covered an entire window of the Logan Drug store; it won the fifty-dollar first prize in a contest. . . . He learned one thing from his prize window: People are impressed by bigness, regardless of content.
—Art Cohn, *The Nine Lives of Michael Todd*

At around the same time, Avrom's family moved to a new home. While helping to fix up the house, he grew annoyed by having to deal with numerous contractors who each did a different job. He thought anyone who could make the home-improvement process easier could earn a good living, so he and his brother Frank founded Atlantic & Pacific Ready Cut Houses, Inc., a company that would function as a middleman between homeowners and various contractors. "President Avrom Goldbogen" built the corporation into a $2 million business while he was still a teenager. Unfortunately, the company's lenders soon went bankrupt—and so did the company.

Seeking a fresh start, Avrom and Bertha moved to Los Angeles. The movie industry there was in the process of converting to sound films. To keep outside noise from creeping into the sound recordings, studios now needed to shoot their films on soundproof stages. Avrom saw an opportunity to put his construction experience to use. By the end of his first week in Los Angeles, he had already contracted to soundproof two studios. As the city grew, Avrom's new construction business took off.

Avrom and Bertha were delighted to have a son, Michael, on October 8, 1929. But when the child was just days old, the stock market crashed, launching the Great Depression. Like many others, Avrom's business collapsed. Further tragedy struck when his father died in 1931. Avrom and Bertha returned to Chicago. For another fresh start, Avrom decided to call himself after his son. As a last name, he chose a variation on his childhood nickname: Todd.

On his 32nd birthday, Avrom Goldbogen legally changed his name to Michael Todd.

In 1933, Mike Todd noticed that Chicago's Century of Progress Exhibition was making money despite the Depression. So he created a show for the exhibition called *The Moth and the Flame*. This provocative dance featured a woman wearing gauzy wings that burned up when she approached a gas flame erupting from center stage. The spectacle proved popular, and Todd loved the publicity and the profits. He realized that audiences were desperate for amusement during hard times, so staying in show business seemed his best chance for success. His first two Broadway plays flopped, but then Todd remembered his school experience. He hired famous tap dancer Bill "Bojangles" Robinson to appear in a jazzy production called *The Hot Mikado*, based on the Gilbert and Sullivan play. It opened in New York City on March 23, 1939, and it was a smash hit.

In 1940, Todd struck it rich with four big attractions at the New York World's Fair, including a 10-acre replica of New Orleans. His next project was the Michael Todd Theater Café in Chicago, which opened on Christmas Day. With room for 8,000 patrons and a 60-foot stage featuring acrobats, dancers, animal trainers, comedy teams, and even a chariot race, the café cemented Todd's new reputation. "At least a few folds of the mantle of P. T. Barnum now flow over the tough shoulders of Showman Mike Todd," declared *Time* magazine.

Todd produced 16 shows during his Broadway career, grossing a total of $18 million. Each one cost an enormous amount of money, and Todd was not afraid to spend. He liked to gamble and lost

As a Broadway producer, Todd worked with many stars of the time, including burlesque dancer Gypsy Rose Lee, actor Mae West, singer Ethel Merman, and the comedy team of Abbott and Costello.

Phineas Taylor Barnum (1810-1891) was a flamboyant showman known for introducing the concept of freak shows and cofounding the famous Barnum and Bailey circus.

more often than he won. Still, he seemed always to find a friend, or even an enemy, to bail him out. "I am often broke, but never poor," Todd declared. The money he made provided him and his wife with everything they wanted, but the two were never a good match, and they finally divorced in 1946. A year later, Todd married actor Joan Blondell. Soon, however, his financial luck deserted him and he was forced into bankruptcy. After he spent Joan's life savings on a failed show, the couple divorced in 1950.

Meanwhile, movie studios were scrambling to find technological marvels to compete with television. In 1951, Todd became interested in Cinerama, a new film exhibition system. Developed by Fred Waller for the 1939 World's Fair, it used three inter-locked cameras, which recorded different sections of the same image on separate strips of film. The three films were then shown on three projectors running simultaneously. Each projected its images onto one-third of a curved screen that was louvered (divided in strips like a venetian blind). Together, they created a wide-angle picture much larger than an ordinary movie. The process was still experimental when Todd discovered it, but he believed it could be his next "big thing," the gimmick that would help him get rich again. He called old friends and convinced them to lend him money to invest in Cinerama.

As soon as Todd could get his hands on a camera, he and Mike Jr. began filming sample footage— including a trip on a gondola in Venice, Italy; Niagara Falls as seen from a helicopter; and a ride on a roller coaster. When *This Is Cinerama* debuted in

During World War II, Waller's system (then using five cameras and known as Vitarama) had been used as a flight simulator to train airplane gunners for combat conditions.

New York on September 30, 1952, the audience was wowed by Todd's work. But despite this promising start, Todd soon sold his stock in the Cinerama Corporation. He knew Cinerama had its limitations. The three-camera setup made filming clumsy. Having three projectors risked imperfect synchronization and color matching between them, and the seams between the three pictures showed. The bulky equipment was too expensive for regular movie theaters and took up valuable seating space. Todd visited Dr. Brian O'Brien, director of the Institute of Optics at the University of Rochester, New York. "Doc," Todd said bluntly, "what I want is Cinerama out of one hole. Can you do it?"

O'Brien replied that creating such a system required the resources of a large company. Todd, however, did not trust big corporations; he wanted to work with O'Brien. Todd pestered O'Brien with

The three images of Venice, Italy, that combined to make one frame of This Is Cinerama

late-night phone calls until he learned that O'Brien had been named vice president of research at the American Optical Company. Todd provided financial support to the company, and O'Brien was placed in charge of Todd's project. In 1953, an army of optical scientists and technicians (including O'Brien's son, Brian O'Brien Jr.) began work on Todd's "Cinerama out of one hole."

In the meantime, competing companies were introducing a flurry of new widescreen processes. The foremost was 20th Century Fox's CinemaScope, which used a special "anamorphic" camera lens to squeeze a wide image onto standard-sized 35-millimeter film. On the projector, another anamorphic lens unsqueezed the image and projected it onto a wide screen. The system's advantage was that it did not require very much special equipment, nor a curved or louvered screen. The first CinemaScope film was the biblical epic *The Robe*, released in September 1953. Fox began leasing its lenses to other companies in 1954, and in a year's time, 20,000 theaters installed wider screens.

CinemaScope had drawbacks, however. The 35mm film could record only so much visual information, and its images lost clarity and brightness when magnified during projection. Also, at about 88 degrees from side to side, the projected picture was far from the full range of human vision (180 degrees). And the aspect ratio—the ratio of width to height—was 2.66:1, twice the normal ratio of 1.33:1. This produced distortions, such as images of faces that seemed too fat. Todd knew he could do better.

They walked into [the office of Walter Stewart, president of American Optical], Pop introduced them, and Mike plunked a certified check for $60,000 down on Walter's desk and said, "Let's talk business." Thus did a 125-year-old New England spectacle maker get thrust into the midst of show business! Talk about culture shock!
—Brian O'Brien Jr.

Henri Chretien developed the first anamorphic lens, which was used in tank and submarine periscopes during World War I.

Other widescreen systems of the early 1950s included Paramount's Vistavision, RKO's SuperScope, Technicolor's Technirama, and Panavision—none of which were truly wide-angle processes.

THE BREAKTHROUGH

Mike Todd was determined that his new system would be as close to full vision as it was possible to get, and it would reach the widest audience possible. To accomplish this, the technicians at American Optical developed a whole series of new processes and devices—from film and cameras to projectors and screens. Almost immediately, they decided that ordinary 35mm film would not do. Not only did the small images become blurry when magnified onto a large screen, but they were also dim because the projector did not let enough light through to illuminate the whole screen. Todd's group eventually decided that its system would use 70mm film: the picture would take up 65mm, and the additional 5mm would hold six stereophonic sound tracks. With much more area for images than 35mm, the large film provided excellent clarity and brightness. The system would also run at 30 frames per second, much faster than the standard 24. This meant increased film costs, but also increased quality. The film was specially designed and manufactured for Todd's project by Eastman Kodak.

Another task was creating a camera lens that could film a more panoramic image. The result of this effort was a huge lens known affectionately as the "Bugeye." Measuring nine inches in diameter and weighing an astonishing 90 pounds, it filmed an image 128 degrees across. It was so sensitive that adjusting it one-sixteenth of an inch changed its depth of focus from four feet to infinity.

In a Los Angeles warehouse, Brian O'Brien Jr. came across some 65mm film equipment that had been used for an old process known as Thomascolor. The American Optical team was able to save many months of work by using the Thomas camera and film perforation device.

If you photograph a cavalry of horses coming toward you and sweeping past using conventional narrow angle lenses (and this includes CinemaScope), the camera never sees the sides of the horses. If this is now projected on a screen, even a wide curved one wrapped around the audience, as the horses go off the screen they all turn facing you and gallop sideways. This is a subtle effect, but the fact that you never see the sides of objects destroys . . . the sense of being in the middle of the action.
—Brian O'Brien Jr.

The team also faced challenges with projection. For an image to look perfect on a wide screen, some distortion must be built into the camera lens. Otherwise, the image would appear normal in the center of the curved screen, but toward either side it would be stretched horizontally. American Optical's technicians designed distortion into the lens so that circular objects (such as faces) would maintain their shape at the sides of the screen as well as at the center. To do so, however, they had to allow some distortion in the way straight lines were projected. The result was that buildings and trees on the sides of the

Brian O'Brien poses with the prototype for the DP70 projector built for Todd's system.

screen bowed inward at the top and the bottom. American Optical devised a way to correct this distortion when printing copies of the film.

The technicians also needed to develop a screen appropriate for their system. The problem was that when light falls on a deeply curved screen, it reflects off one side of the screen onto the other, washing out the images. Cinerama had solved this by using a louvered screen, but it was fragile and too expensive for ordinary movie theaters. Todd's team wanted to design a screen that was wide and curved, but could still hang on a standard frame. The result was known as a lenticular screen—vinyl-coated fabric with an aluminum surface, covered with many tiny mirrors that were positioned at different angles to prevent the light from reflecting back onto the screen.

Finally, there was the issue of what to call this new system. Todd declared it would be no "-rama" or "-scope," because audiences were already confused by the array of widescreen systems. Instead, he wanted it to be called the Todd Process or the O'Brien Process. American Optical objected: "It seems only fair that it should contain some reference to our firm." "Agreed," Todd said. "We can call it Todd-AO." Although it was O'Brien who had developed the widescreen technology, the optician believed the name was an apt one: "It is due to [Todd's] vision and imagination, plus his drive and determination to stay with it during the difficult period of development, that it came into being," he said. "I am glad that the process has his name on it."

As with Cinerama, Todd quickly made a test film with his new system that featured spectacular footage such as a ride on a rollercoaster and a gondola tour of Venice. When the film was shown to members of the press, it was so vivid that one reviewer became seasick and had to leave. "We were sure that he would give it a bad review, but on the contrary he raved about the process," Brian O'Brien Jr. recalled.

THE RESULT

The completed Todd-AO system offered the wrap-around feeling of Cinerama, but with less expensive equipment and with better picture and sound quality. It was designed to help filmmakers tell sweeping, theatrical stories in which viewers felt like part of the action. When it was introduced in 1955 with the film version of the Broadway musical *Oklahoma!*, Todd-AO became an instant sensation. The wide screen was a perfect medium for big musical production numbers set against acres of corn. The uniqueness of the film was matched by its presentation. Mike Todd insisted that Todd-AO movies would be referred to as "shows" to emphasize that they were unique attractions. They would play in only about 100 theaters in 50 major cities, and with just a few showings per day, tickets (presold at higher prices and with reserved seating) would always be in high demand. To maintain a classier atmosphere, Todd even banned popcorn from theaters that played his shows. This strategy, combined with Todd-AO's grandiose new widescreen system, made *Oklahoma!* a hit with both critics and audiences.

Todd had been disappointed when he was not granted creative control of *Oklahoma!*, and despite the film's success, he believed it failed to use Todd-AO's full capabilities. His next project was designed to show the process to its best advantage, and he managed the entire production. His film, *Around the World in 80 Days* (based on the classic Jules Verne novel), took a year and a half to cast, shoot, and edit.

A strip of Todd-AO film from Oklahoma! Ironically, the innovative Bugeye lens was barely used in the movie. Unaccustomed to thinking in widescreen and unsure how to use the enormous new lens, the filmmakers had insisted that Todd-AO also provide smaller lenses. They promised these would be used only for closeups, but in the end they used them for all but two scenes.

Mike Todd stands next to the Todd-AO camera (fitted with the Bugeye lens) while working on a scene from Around the World in 80 Days.

It cost the then-astronomical sum of $6 million, and no wonder: it featured 50 stars filmed in 13 different countries. The costumes numbered nearly 75,000. For a bullfight sequence, Todd used the entire population of the town of Chinchon, Spain—more than 4,000 people. When *Around the World in 80 Days* was released on October 17, 1956, it cemented Todd's reputation as a showman. The film made $16 million, was nominated for nine Academy Awards, and won five of them, including Best Picture. Another Todd-AO film version of a Broadway musical, *South*

Pacific (1957), was also a success. In 1957, the Todd-AO Corporation was presented with an Academy Award for its revolutionary process.

At what seemed to be the height of his success in the motion-picture industry, Todd was also happy in his personal life. In 1956, he began a well-publicized relationship with actor Elizabeth Taylor, who was widely regarded as one of the most beautiful women in the world. Not only was Taylor younger than Todd's son, but she was also married (although legally separated) when the two began courting. Taylor married Todd on February 2, 1957, and the couple's daughter, Elizabeth Frances, was born on August 5. Tragically, however, Mike Todd was killed when his private plane, the *Lucky Liz*, crashed in New Mexico on March 22, 1958. He had been on his way to New York City to attend a dinner party at the Waldorf-Astoria Hotel, given in his honor. Elizabeth Taylor had stayed home with a fever.

After Todd's death, 20th Century Fox bought the rights to the Todd-AO process and produced more films, including the classics *Cleopatra* (1963)—which starred Elizabeth Taylor—*The Sound of Music* (1965), and *Hello, Dolly!* (1969). Only 18 feature films were ever made in Todd-AO, but they were so successful that they won a total of 18 Academy Awards and grossed more than $260 million. Although the process is no longer in use, film critics and audiences agree that none of these timeless movies would have had the blockbusting effect on audiences that they did—and still do—without the magic of Todd-AO.

Taylor and Todd together in 1957

CHAPTER SEVEN

Garrett Brown
and the Steadicam

Early motion-picture cameras were heavy and unwieldy, much like early photographic cameras. The first movies were filmed as though they were stage plays—with the camera standing still, centered before the action, like a member of the audience. Eventually, directors learned how editing, special effects, and camera movement could make films different from plays. Today, movies and television nearly always use tracking shots (camera movement forward and backward or side to side) and booming (camera movement up and down) to establish settings, follow the movements of actors, and point the viewer's attention where the director wants it. Modern audiences are so accustomed to watching moving shots that they hardly notice camera movement at all. But when Garrett Brown was making TV commercials in the early 1970s, moving the camera was still quite a trick. Lighter, handheld cameras had been invented, but they produced jittery

Within a few years of its invention, the camera-movement system created by Garrett Brown (b. 1942) became a standard tool in filming nearly all motion pictures and many television shows.

shots, as the small, constant movements of the operator's body translated to the film. Brown became determined to change all that. His invention of "a graceful way to hold the camera, as a weightless object balanced on the tips of your fingers," allowed pictures to move in a way they never had before.

Garrett Brown was born in 1942. He was two years old when his father, a chemist at DuPont Corporation, invented a new adhesive for paperback book bindings that is still used today. Partly because of his father's ingenuity, Garrett grew up in what he later called "a curious and inventive atmosphere based on old Yankee traditions." Some of his ancestors were railroad engineers, and he came to believe that "there are a few genes knocking around in there that help me with mechanics." When Garrett was nine years old, he suffered from nephritis, an inflammation of the kidneys. Staying in bed for months, he kept himself busy reading the entire *World Book Encyclopedia* and designing "silly inventions" that he sketched in a notebook.

After high school, Garrett Brown attended Tufts University on a Navy scholarship. But soon he and a friend, Al Dana, got together as a folk-music duo and dropped out of college to go on the road. For three years, Brown & Dana made a decent living playing college concerts and folk clubs, as well as recording for MGM. "It was a great young man's job," Brown said later. "I thought showbiz was going to be it for me for life." Then a serious auto accident caused the band to miss gigs; it broke up in 1964.

"Souls with some creativity but with no particular qualifications could get into advertising in the '60s," Brown remembered. He spent several years as a copywriter at an ad agency. There, he met Anne Winn, with whom he recorded a number of radio commercials—mainly released in the 1970s and 1980s—for large clients such as Kodak, American Express, and Molson. Being a radio voice was a fun sideline, but it was not where Brown's true talents lay. Instead, he became interested in filming. He "read my way through the 30-foot shelf of film books at the Philadelphia Library," and this knowledge proved useful in making television commercials. Brown produced many award-winning spots for the ad agency, but he decided that what he really wanted to do was start his own production company and direct commercials himself. In 1969, he did just that.

Brown bought bargain equipment from a production company that was going out of business. One piece he obtained was an 800-pound Fearless Panoram Dolly (a heavy car designed to move a camera) and a track (rails for the car to roll on). "It was a wonderfully smooth dolly," Brown remembered, "but it was a pain in the neck." Still, he didn't want to give up moving the camera to shoot his commercials. "It offended some deep part of me inherited from my inventing ancestors that I couldn't move a camera stably without putting this contraption under it," he said. "We broke our hearts lugging this dolly around in pickup trucks and laying it on my rusty rails but I loved the moving camera. I think I'm a moving-camera junky. I love this two-dimensional

Inventing is a job that is misperceived by most people. It's mostly about identifying the gaps in your life that might be filled by something. People take for granted and gloss over the gaps, the missing things. My clue that something is worth working on is if I really want one myself. I'm not into inventing things that one thinks can be sold to other people. It's somewhat unreliable and you can break your heart and lose money. But if you really want one and you figure it out, the worst case is that you at least own one. The rest of it is just dogged hard work, trying every damn thing you can think of and a willingness to spend your own money.
—Garrett Brown

A dolly being used to move a camera and microphone on a movie set in the 1940s

medium when it has the illusion of three-dimensionality." There must be a better way, Brown thought. He wanted a device that combined the stable, smooth images of a dolly with the freedom of a handheld camera.

For decades, using a tripod (a three-legged stand) had been the only way to keep motion-picture cameras stable. As early as 1910, tripod cameras had been fitted with movable heads that allowed them to pan (rotate from side to side) and tilt (rotate up and down). Dollies, which could move the camera forward and backward, began to be used in 1912. By 1929, cameras could also be mounted on a crane—a large trolley with a long projecting arm, at the end of which was a platform on which the camera and operator stood. In addition to creating overhead shots, cranes could combine several camera movements (such as panning and booming) simultaneously.

All this equipment was still cumbersome, however, and filmmakers kept seeking more freedom of movement. The earliest camera designed for handheld use was the Moy Gyro in 1911. It was not made for the filmmakers who supplied the new movie theaters, but for the navy to conduct aerial surveillance from hydrogen blimps. The camera was stabilized by an electric gyroscope, a heavy, quickly spinning wheel mounted in a frame so that it could turn freely in any direction, thus keeping its balance despite the position of its support. The Moy Gyro's special hand grips allowed the operator to hold the camera away from his or her body, providing additional stability and less bumpy footage, even under combat conditions. The Moy Gyro was the best handheld camera available until the invention of the Askania in Germany in 1938. The Askania rested on the operator's shoulder while he or she looked through an eyepiece.

The advent of television in the 1950s intensified the need for efficient portable cameras, since news reporting required the ability to film at any location with speed and agility. Lighter cameras were developed, as well as useful new accessories. In 1955, the Helivision anti-vibration helicopter mount was introduced. This mount attached a motion-picture camera to a gimbal (similar to a gyroscope). Among the smooth aerial shots made possible by the Helivision mount was the famous opening sequence of *The Sound of Music* (1965). Another improvement was the hydraulic crab dolly. With the ability to move in any direction (side to side as well as front to back) and elevate the camera noiselessly up to six feet off the ground at any speed, it overcame at least some of the traditional dolly's limitations. Despite these and other innovations, however, camera movement could still be clumsy and limited.

So when Garrett Brown wanted to move his camera without breaking his back, he had to design his own contraptions. To shoot through the windows of a moving car in commercials for Subaru, one of his clients, he developed the "Coptercam"—a camera that hung from a ball that itself hung 30 feet below a helicopter. More advanced than the Helivision mount, Brown's rig kept the camera stable alongside the moving vehicle.

One of the first movies to use the Helivision mount was *The Red Balloon* (1955), which followed the adventures of a balloon as it blew from place to place. For this film, new technology did not simply help the director interpret the script; it inspired the script itself (which won an Academy Award for Best Original Screenplay). The story would have been impossible to film without a device that allowed the camera to shoot from a balloon's "point of view."

Next, Brown devised the "Pole Rig": a pole with a crossbar and a couple of weights for balance. The camera operator held the pole with the camera mounted on it. This setup was surprisingly stable, Brown discovered. But he still could not get shots to move from low to high, for example, because the camera tilted when the pole was lifted. "I suppose if I had been satisfied with this gadget . . . the project would have ultimately fizzled, but I couldn't quite leave it alone," Brown said. So, in the spring of 1973, he attached a camera to a miniature aluminum crane that weighed only 70 pounds. This revised Pole Rig allowed the camera to pan and tilt, in addition to being carried steadily from place to place. The new device produced beautiful shots, but it was still far too heavy. "We hired the biggest, strongest cameramen in the land and sent them all home in a pillowcase after a day with the 'Pole Rig!'" joked Brown. He tried a mechanism of bungee cords and pulleys to support the weight of the camera, but he had to admit it was "wildly impractical in the end," mostly because the device was so huge "it wouldn't fit through narrow places in the set."

Brown kept his inventions quiet by requiring his clients to sign secrecy agreements. He wanted to perfect his devices before anyone knew how he got such amazing shots. He needed time to think without any distractions, so he checked into a motel. For weeks, Brown lived on room service while "balancing brooms on his fingers, dashing out to hardware stores and studying old drawings." Finally, looking at a desk lamp gave him an idea.

Garrett Brown with his Pole Rig

THE BREAKTHROUGH

Brown needed a device that could accomplish three things: isolating the camera from the operator's body to keep shots steady, shifting its center of gravity to keep it from tilting when the operator walked, and distributing its weight so that it could be moved easily. His solution to the first two problems was to use an arm that was jointed and flexible, like the desk lamp, to hold the camera away from the operator. The arm's two joints would allow it—and the camera—to move up and down, left and right, and toward and away from the subject. At the same time, the camera operator could also be in motion, walking or even running. A gimbal kept the camera steady during movement.

In addition to allowing a wide range of smooth movement, Brown's invention reduced strain on the operator. The arm was attached to the operator by a vest that distributed the camera's weight evenly over the shoulders, back, and hips. Rather than struggling to keep his or her eyes trained on a tiny eyepiece to see what was being filmed, the operator used a fiber-optic viewfinder, a small tube that was held in front of the eye by a headband. (Later versions of the invention had video monitors instead.)

Brown emerged from the motel with sketches and a plan for his "Brown Stabilizer." Now he had to get the thing built. He collected parts, wheedled friends and acquaintances with tools and the skill to help, and "had the thing ready to test within about two months." Brown's prototype, patented in 1975, weighed an astonishingly light 23 pounds. He quickly set about showing what it could do. "I filmed a five-minute demo," he recalled. "I shot all over Philadelphia, jumping up on boxes, moving through doorways and traffic, and I even ran up and down the steps of the Philadelphia Art Museum."

Brown then made an appointment at Cinema Products Corporation, a Los Angeles company he hoped would manufacture and market the device. The morning of the meeting, he went to the laboratory that had developed his film and saw his footage for the first time. "Every shot on the reel is impossible and revolutionary," Brown later recalled with

Brown demonstrates a prototype of his "stabilizer" in 1973

glee. "Nearly twenty different, never-before-seen camera stunts on one reel and not one could have been made with any known combination of dolly and crane." After watching the film once, the lab's amazed projectionist said, "What was that?" and ran it again, then called in his boss and other employees to see it. The response at Cinema Products was just as favorable. The company's president, Ed DiGiulio, immediately agreed to purchase the invention and begin production. Only one thing was unacceptable to Cinema Products: the name. Instead of the Brown Stabilizer, the device became the Steadicam.

The Steadicam made shots so smooth, they looked as though they were done with a dolly, even in places where a dolly could not travel or would be almost impossible to set up. An article in *American Cinematographer* described its remarkable potential in the hands of skilled operator: "The Steadicam can reverse its direction rapidly and without any visible bump in the shot so one can back into a doorway or alcove and push out again as the actors pass by camera. In addition, since there are no . . . handles in the way and no need for an operator's eye on the viewfinder, one can pass the camera within an inch of walls or door frames. The combination makes a formidable tool for shooting in tight location spaces." In addition, the Steadicam was ideal for shooting over rough ground or long distances; moving through doorways or up stairs; running or falling; traveling on skis, skates, horses, or vehicles; representing a person or animal's point of view; and capturing quick, unpredictable moments.

Brown later claimed that he had put himself so heavily in debt for his new device that he had trouble getting his demo film back from the laboratory because his account was past due. He took a gamble and asked the lab employees to take a look at the footage and see what they thought. They agreed and were supposedly so impressed that they released Brown's print for his meeting at Cinema Products. In 1988, Brown admitted, "Maybe I made this up in some interview, but so what? It doesn't matter—it's still plenty exciting!"

You're tucking into corners and the camera is on one side of you and then the other side and the viewer [of the finished film] has no idea where the operator is.
—Garrett Brown

Even after the Steadicam had been perfected and mass produced by Cinema Products, Garrett Brown was the only person who knew how to use it. He was soon in demand as a Steadicam operator on feature films. Here, on a set designed to look like a migrant worker camp during the Great Depression, he shoots a scene for Bound for Glory *(1976).*

THE RESULT

The industry's reaction to the Steadicam, much like the amazed lab projectionist's, was positive. Directors who saw Brown's demo footage jumped at the chance to use the new technology. In 1975, Brown was hired to use the Steadicam to shoot scenes for two feature motion pictures to be released in 1976. In *Bound for Glory*, starring David Carradine as the folk singer Woody Guthrie, Brown demonstrated his invention's capabilities by filming a four-minute-long shot that required him to start atop a 30-foot-high crane, slowly descend to ground level, and then walk alongside Carradine. For *Marathon Man*, Brown jogged for miles while filming Dustin Hoffman, who played a runner.

Director John Avildsen also saw Brown's demo film, and he loved the footage in which Brown pursued his wife, Ellen, down and back up the steps of the Philadelphia Art Museum. Avildsen happened to be directing a movie, written by and starring the then-unknown Sylvester Stallone, that was set in Philadelphia. He decided to hire Brown to film some of the scenes for *Rocky*, which went on to win

Brown gets up close to the action while filming a boxing scene for Rocky.

Brown holds his Steadicam in "low mode" during the filming of The Shining *at Borehamwood Studios in England. "I began the picture with years of Steadicam use behind me and with the assumption that I could do whatever anyone could reasonably demand," he later recalled. "I realized by the afternoon of the first day's work that here was a whole new ball game, and that the word 'reasonable' was not in Kubrick's lexicon."*

the Academy Award for Best Picture of 1976. The Steadicam was used in boxing sequences, as well as in one of the movie's most famous shots: Stallone running up the art museum steps.

In 1977, Garrett Brown and Cinema Products accepted an Academy Award for technical achievement in inventing and developing the Steadicam. Brown then spent much of 1979 filming scenes for Stanley Kubrick's horror film *The Shining*. Kubrick was such a demanding director and the scenes were so challenging that Brown later referred to the experience as "the Steadicam Olympics." The footage he shot included the "Big Wheel" scenes that followed a child pedaling at high speed up and down hotel hallways, as well as the climactic chase sequence through a hedge maze. When it was released in 1980, *The Shining* cemented industry approval of Brown's new marvel. The Steadicam was used in nearly every feature film production after that. Its ease of use in the hands of a trained operator, as well as the almost limitless choices it gave to a director, ensured its success.

Brown, no stranger to finding a way to get the right shot, worked on a number of other innovative cameras. He used his newly invented Mobycam, a camera that could follow swimmers underwater, to film portions of the 1992 Olympics for broadcast by NBC. Brown then helped film the 1996 Olympics with his DiveCam, which followed divers as they dropped into the water; GoCam, which shot events such as track, fencing, wrestling, gymnastics, and soccer; and SkyCam, which captured the opening and closing ceremonies from the air. In 1998, Brown

Garrett Brown with his SkyCam

accepted another Academy Award, this time with his colleague Jerry Holway, for the creation of the Skyman elevated platform for Steadicam operators. Brown also continued to work as a Steadicam operator—on nearly 200 movies. In addition, he instructed others in how to use his invention.

Aware of the changing technologies of the motion-picture industry, Brown expected his invention to become obsolete: "I thought some kind of black box with a 'stabilizer' button might come along and knock Steadicam out of the ring." Instead, his Steadicam remains one of the most popular and indispensable inventions in film history.

In 1997, Garrett Brown estimated that he had taught about 1,000 Steadicam operators worldwide—including his son, Jonathan, who became a professional cameraman.

Films of the Future

W hen cable television, satellite broadcasting, and videocassette recorders (VCRs) appeared in the late 1970s, film industry insiders feared the worst: the extinction of movie theaters. Since people could now watch films at home, why would they pay for movie tickets? Studios began to make fewer films, but they spent more on each one in an attempt to draw the widest possible audience to theaters.

Despite the fears of studio executives, cable television networks and VCRs actually extended the life of a movie indefinitely. "In the 1930s," notes author Richard Rickitt, "a film was considered a 'spent' product within two years of its release." But the huge audience that watched the network television broadcast of *Gone with the Wind* in 1976 proved that people were still interested in seeing older films. Today, movies are broadcast on pay-per-view, cable, and network television, as well as being released on video and digital video disk (DVD). All these outlets

Motion pictures continued to evolve in the late twentieth century. One innovation was the IMAX system, which projected films on gigantic screens that seemed to surround the audience.

allow studios to make more money from a single film.

Still, the movie industry did change in some ways after VCRs and cable television became popular. As part of the plan to attract wider audiences, neighborhood movie theaters with only one screen, showing a single film, gave way to the shopping-mall multiscreen cineplexes so common today. These allowed potential ticket buyers a choice of many different movies and showtimes at a single site. During the same period, ticket prices began to increase to offset the costs of swelling movie budgets.

Filmmakers also continued their efforts to make movie screens so huge and sound so clear that viewers felt as though they were experiencing reality, not just a film. In 1967, giant-screen films shown on multiple projectors were a big hit at the Montreal Exposition. A trio of Canadian entrepreneurs who had made some of these films—Graeme Ferguson, Robert Kerr, and Roman Kroitor—decided to develop a new giant-screen system that used a single projector. Their system, called IMAX, used screens up to eight stories high and six-track multispeaker sound systems. The film itself was huge, three times larger than Todd-AO and ten times larger than ordinary 35mm. It was advanced horizontally through the most powerful projectors ever built, which used a vacuum to hold film right up to the lens for superior focus. IMAX debuted in Osaka, Japan, in 1970, and the first permanent IMAX theater opened in Toronto in 1971. An IMAX Dome (known as OMNIMAX) with an even larger, more rounded screen opened in San Diego two years later; IMAX 3D was introduced in 1986. By 2003, there were more than 220 IMAX theaters in 30 countries. The IMAX Corporation received Academy Awards in 1985 and 1996 for its innovative system.

New formats such as DVD and advances in exhibition technology such as IMAX definitely changed the way audiences experienced movies. But the biggest area of innovation in the late twentieth century was in visual-effects technology. The real breakthrough began in 1977 with *Star Wars*. Written and directed by George Lucas, *Star Wars* was the first motion picture that was advertised as an attraction because of its effects. Lines formed

Another new technology was IMAX DMR (Digital Re-Mastering), which could convert any live-action 35mm film into IMAX format. Movies shown in IMAX DMR included *Apollo 13, Star Wars Episode II: Attack of the Clones, The Matrix Reloaded,* and *The Matrix Revolutions* (the first Hollywood film to be released simultaneously in 35mm and IMAX formats).

George Lucas (left) with his friend Steven Spielberg. Spielberg was also a pioneer director of blockbusters featuring extensive visual effects, including Jaws (1975), Close Encounters of the Third Kind (1977), and E. T.: The Extra-Terrestrial (1982).

around the block at movie theaters across the nation (hence the term "blockbuster" to describe a wildly successful film that attracts a wide variety of people).

Previously, Hollywood studios had kept their visual-effects techniques secret for fear of destroying the "magic" that attracted audiences. Now, since the effects themselves were drawing audiences, books and articles were published about visual-effects technology, sparking public fascination that brought in even bigger audiences. After Lucas released a successful sequel to *Star Wars* in 1980, he decided to make his temporary visual-effects production company, Industrial Light & Magic (ILM), permanent. It went on to become a leader in the field, winning nearly a dozen Academy Awards.

For the filming of the fast-paced spaceship battles in the *Star Wars* films, visual-effects supervisor John Dykstra created a computer-operated camera. Before the "Dykstraflex," as it became known, the scenes would probably have been filmed using small, detailed models of spaceships that were moved using wires or other devices. The technique was time-consuming and laborious, and it risked the wires or other devices being seen on the finished film. Instead of moving the models, the Dykstraflex camera moved around them. Its intricate movements were programmed into a computer, so they could be repeated exactly and endlessly. This method was not only efficient, but it also created images that looked more realistic. Since the camera moved quickly around the models with its shutter open, it recorded images that were blurred in the way that

John Dykstra won an Academy Award for his special-effects work on *Star Wars* and a Scientific and Technical Academy Award for the development of the ILM facility.

actual fast-moving objects appear to be. After its successful use in *Star Wars*, the computerized camera became a cornerstone of visual-effects technique.

Camera movement controlled by a computer was impressive, but the real innovation came when computers themselves began producing images. The 1982 Disney film *TRON*—the story of a computer programmer transported into his computer, where the video games he invented came to life—was the first to use several minutes of computer-generated footage. Although the film flopped, subsequent movies helped make computer-generated imagery (CGI) extremely popular. *Star Trek II: The Wrath of Khan* (1982), for example, contained the first entirely computer-generated sequence in any feature film. Its use of the technology to show a barren moon evolving into a lush planet helped make the new worlds it portrayed seem real.

In the early 1990s, computer imaging experienced a major technological breakthrough. CGI had previously been put on film using devices, such as Linwood Dunn's optical printer, that filmed a projected computer image. This technique worked, but it resulted in some loss of picture quality. New scanning and recording technology, however, allowed film images to be converted into digital data, moved or changed as necessary on a computer, and put back onto film—with no loss of picture quality. Some of the first and most influential films using this new technology were *Terminator 2: Judgment Day* (1991), with a liquid-metal character who could morph into

A digital-effects scene from Terminator 2, *created by ILM*

Toy Story took four years to make and took up 1,000 gigabytes of data.

anything, and *Jurassic Park* (1993), featuring computer-generated dinosaurs interacting with people.

In 1995 came another breakthrough: a new film that was entirely computer-generated. Pixar, a company that had once been the digital research and development division of Industrial Light & Magic, released its debut feature film, *Toy Story*. It was a smash hit, and Pixar went on to make other CGI films, including *A Bug's Life* (1998) and *Monsters, Inc.* (2001). But CGI was soon used in most live-action films, as well. In the 1994 film *Forrest Gump*, special-effects artists used computers to place an actor's face and figure in historical films—so that Tom Hanks could seem to shake hands with President John F. Kennedy, for example. After that, when effects artists needed to add a person or thing to an image, they could "Gump it in." For example, large crowd scenes, which used to require hundreds of extras and costumes, could now be "filmed" by computer.

In 1999, another groundbreaking film showed the potential of CGI to change the entire movie industry. In *Star Wars Episode I: The Phantom Menace*, the long-awaited "prequel" to George Lucas's original trilogy, CGI was used to develop entirely digital

ILM employees work on computer-generated visual effects for the film The Perfect Storm *(2000).*

128

characters who interacted with human actors. Lucas
also used computer imaging to "touch up" actors'
facial expressions and even change dialogue after the
shooting was done. Such innovations caused people
to wonder if computer-generated images would one
day replace actors.

Watching the technological marvels showcased
in recent films, it is hard to imagine how miraculous
the first motion pictures must have seemed. The
incredible opportunities offered by the early film
industry seem unreal today. Nearly anyone with a
bit of money and some imagination—such as George
Méliès or D. W. Griffith—could acquire or invent
filmmaking equipment to make crowd-pleasing,
artistic, and profitable entertainment. As filmmaking
began to require more specialized and expensive
equipment, including advanced cameras, sound-
recording technology, color film, visual-effects
devices, and dollies and cranes, it became harder for
new people to break into the movie business.

But has filmmaking come full circle since its
birth more than a century ago? "Independent"
films—produced outside the major Hollywood studio system—became increasingly popular after the
mid-1980s. The unprecedented success of the 1999
film *The Blair Witch Project*, which was shot in digital
video (DV) and 16mm film and advertised heavily on
the Internet, seemed to show how nearly anyone
could become a filmmaker. The free-for-all that
characterized the early days of motion pictures
seemed to be happening again, thanks to relatively
inexpensive new technology. With a little money,

digital video (DV): a video
format that records images
and soundtrack in digital
form so that they can be
imported into and edited on
a computer

even an amateur could purchase a small, lightweight, image-stabilized DV camera, along with a personal computer and editing software.

Observers of these new devices wondered if people would even go to the movies in the future. Although expensive film stock still offered the best picture quality and longevity, some industry insiders eagerly anticipated its extinction in favor of DV. Streaming Web-based video, some people believed, might replace movie theaters by allowing potential ticket buyers to stay home and download whichever films they chose. John Bailey, in an article for the International Cinematographers Guild, compared these advances to the invention of motion pictures themselves. Describing his reaction to watching an early Kinetoscope film at a museum, he wrote, "Eyes pressed close to the viewer, the flickering, stamp-size image . . . reminded me of nothing as much as trying to watch a webfilm on your computer. Truly, this is the very birth of a new medium."

Whatever the possibilities, motion pictures, having taken more than 100 years to develop, are not likely to disappear anytime soon. Television, cable networks, videocassettes, DVDs, and the Internet have not been able to kill them. Chances are, whatever the entertainments of the future look like, people will still go out to the movies. Like the first few dozen who walked into the Salon Indien in December 1895 to see the Lumière brothers' debut of projected motion pictures, they'll buy tickets to sit in a dark room and stare at a screen, hoping to be amazed, educated, and entertained.

GLOSSARY

additive color: a color film production technique in which color is added during projection (usually by colored filters)

anamorphic lens: a lens that squeezes a wide image onto standard-sized film and unsqueezes it for projection onto a wide screen

aperture: the opening in the front of a camera through which light passes when a picture is taken

aspect ratio: the ratio of image width to height (usually 1.33:1 in motion-picture theaters)

back projection: a visual effect in which a background scene is projected onto a screen behind actors so that it appears they are actually in the location being shown

blue-screen photography: a visual effect in which a subject is filmed in front of a brightly colored screen, which is later replaced with a separately filmed background scene

booming: camera movement up and down

celluloid: a colorless, flammable, plastic-like substance used to make photographic film

cinema: a motion-picture theater; also, the art of motion pictures

cinematography: motion-picture photography

computer-generated imagery (CGI): images that originate from a computer rather than being filmed in real life, or images that are greatly enhanced using a computer

crane: a trolley with a long projecting arm to support and move a camera

digital video (DV): a video format that records images and soundtrack in digital form so that they can be imported into and edited on a computer

dissolve: an editing technique in which one shot is gradually replaced by another

dolly: a heavy car that carries a motion-picture camera along a track to capture smooth moving shots

130

dye transfer printing: a color film production technique in which color from dyed strips of film is printed onto a special clear film called the base

emulsion: a mixture of chemicals; in photography, a mixture of light-sensitive chemicals applied to film

fade: an editing technique in which the screen gradually changes from black to image (fade in) or from image to black (fade out)

fiber-optics: bundles of thin glass fibers through which light (and images) can travel

film: a slim, flexible material coated with light-sensitive chemicals

filter: a colored screen that controls the amount and type of light that passes through it; a green filter, for instance, blocks out all colors of light except green

frame: one individual image on a strip of motion-picture film

gimbal: a device that stays level despite the position of its support

glass shot: a visual effect in which a detailed painting on a large piece of glass is used to alter or extend real scenery

gyroscope: a spinning wheel mounted in a frame so that it can turn freely in any direction, thus keeping its balance despite the position of its support

Latham loop: a loop between each reel of film and the lens of a projector, designed to keep the film from breaking

lens: a curved piece of glass used to change the direction of light rays

magic lantern: a device that projected still images by shining light through drawings or photographs on pieces of glass

matte shot: a visual effect in which a mask is used to cover part of the camera lens during filming, keeping portions of the film unexposed so that separate images can be added later

multiple exposure: a visual effect in which more than one image is photographed onto the same piece of film

negative: a film image that shows light and dark, and right and left, reversed; a camera records a negative, and then positive prints are developed from it

optical printer: a device combining a motion-picture camera and projector to make copies of film prints; also used to create many visual effects

optical sound: a method of creating sound films by converting sound into light and recording it on film

pan: camera rotation from side to side

patent: government recognition that an invention belongs to a particular inventor, which gives the inventor the sole right to produce and sell the invention for the duration of the patent

perforations: the series of holes along the edges of a strip of film

persistence of vision: a phenomenon allowing the eye to continue to see a picture for a split second after it disappears, thus making a rapid series of still images seem like continuous motion

phonograph: a machine that used a needle to play back sound recorded on a grooved, rotating cylinder or disk; invented by Thomas Edison in 1877

positive: a photograph or film produced from a negative that shows light and dark, and right and left, as seen in reality; also called a print

prism: a piece of glass that splits a single beam of light into two or more beams

reel: a frame that holds film, revolving to unwind or rewind it during filming or projection

shutter: a mechanism that alternately opens and closes to admit and block light in a camera or projector

sprockets: clawed gears in a camera or projector that pull film forward by its perforations

stereophonic sound: a sound system in which multiple soundtracks are used to re-create sound realistically in different locations around the audience

stop-motion animation: a visual effect in which a miniature figure is photographed one frame at a time as it is moved in extremely small increments; when the film is run at its regular speed, the figure appears to be moving

substitution shot: a visual effect in which filming is stopped while a person or object is substituted for another person or object, whereupon filming resumes

three-dimensional (3-D): images that appear to have depth, as well as height and width; 3-D motion pictures seem to emerge from the screen toward the audience

tilt: camera rotation up and down

tracking shot: camera movement from side to side or forward and backward

tripod: a three-legged stand used to support a camera

visual effect: any technique used to create the illusion of something onscreen that did not actually happen during filming; also called a special effect

wipe: an editing technique in which one shot appears to be pushed off the screen by another shot

zoom lens: a lens that can gradually change focus to make it appear that the camera is moving closer to a subject

BIBLIOGRAPHY

American Society of Cinematographers. "In Memoriam: Linwood G. Dunn, ASC." www.theasc.com/clubhouse/inside/memoriam/dunn.htm.

Basten, Fred E. *Glorious Technicolor: The Movies' Magic Rainbow*. Cranbury, N.J.: A. S. Barnes, 1980.

Belton, John. "Todd-AO: The Show of Shows." *In 70mm: The 70mm Newsletter*, November 2001. http://hjem.get2net.dk/in70mm/magazine.backissues/2001/66/show_of_shows/show.htm.

Biograph Company website. www.biographcompany.com.

Brown, Garrett. "Ancient History." *Steadicam Letter*, December 1988. www.steadicam.ca/mainfile/article/history/anc.html.

———. "The Iron Age." *Steadicam Letter*, March 1989. www.steadicam.ca/mainfile/article/history/iron.html.

———. "A Note from Steadicam Inventor Garrett Brown." www.steadicam.ca/mainfile/article/anote/anote.html.

———. "The Steadicam and The Shining." www.visual-memory.co.uk/sk/ac/page2.htm.

Carneal, Georgette. *A Conqueror of Space: An Authorized Biography of the Life and Work of Lee de Forest*. New York: Horace Liveright, 1930.

Ceram, C. W. *Archaeology of Cinema*. Transl. Richard Winston. New York: Harcourt, Brace, 1965.

Cercel, Elif. "Dunn Dies, Magic Lives On." *VFXPro*, May 27, 1998.

Coe, Brian. *The History of Movie Photography*. Westfield, N.J.: Eastview Editions, 1981.

Cohn, Art. *The Nine Lives of Michael Todd*. New York: Random House, 1958.

Comer, Brooke. "Steadicam Hits Its Stride." *American Cinematographer*, June 1992. www.steadicam.ca/mainfile/article/Garrett1/Garrett.html.

Cook, David. *A History of Narrative Film*. New York: Norton, 1981.

Crafton, Donald. *The Talkies: American Cinema's Transition to Sound, 1926-1931*. New York: Scribner's, 1997.

Daly, James, ed. "Hollywood 2.0." *Wired*, November 1997. www.wired.com/wired/archive/5.11/hollywood_pr.html.

Daly, Steve. "Faking It." *Entertainment Weekly*, August 16, 2002.

de Forest, Lee. *Father of Radio: The Autobiography of Lee de Forest*. Chicago: Wilcox & Follett, 1950.

Dickson, W. K. L., and Antonia Dickson. *History of the Kinetograph, Kinetoscope, and Kinetophonograph* (1895). New York: Arno, 1970.

Dunn, Linwood G., ed., et. al. *The ASC Treasury of Visual Effects*. Hollywood: American Society of Cinematographers, 1983.

Eastman Kodak Company. "History of Kodak." www.kodak.com/US/en/corp/aboutKodak/kodakHistory/kodakHistory.shtml.

Eberle, Ed. "Garrett Brown: Steadicam Inventor." *Film & Video*, October 1999.

Eyman, Scott. *The Speed of Sound: Hollywood and the Talkie Revolution, 1926-1930*. New York: Simon & Schuster, 1997.

Ferrara, Serena. *Steadicam: Techniques and Aesthetics*. Oxford: Focal, 2001.

Fielding, Raymond, ed. *A Technological History of Motion Pictures and Television: An Anthology from the Pages of the Journal of the Society of Motion Picture and Television Engineers*. Berkeley: University of California, 1967.

Finch, Christopher. *Special Effects: Creating Movie Magic*. New York: Abbeville, 1984.

Gabler, Neal. *An Empire of Their Own: How the Jews Invented Hollywood.* New York: Crown, 1988.

Gomery, J. Douglas. *The Coming of Sound to American Cinema: A History of the Transformation of an Industry.* Ann Arbor, Mich.: University Microfilms International, 1984.

Haines, Richard W. *Technicolor Movies: The History of Dye Transfer Printing.* Jefferson, N.C.: McFarland, 1993.

Hamilton, Jake. *Special Effects in Film and Television.* New York: DK, 1998.

Hecht, Jeff. "The Amazing Optical Adventures of Todd-AO." *In 70mm: The 70mm Newsletter*, March 2002. http://hjem.get2net.dk/in70mm/magazine/backissues/2002/67/optical_adventure/adventure.htm.

Hendricks, Gordon. *The Edison Motion Picture Myth.* Berkeley: University of California, 1961.

IMAX Corporation. "Corporate Profile." www.imax.com/corporate/content/corporate/intro.html.

Institut Lumière website. www.institut-lumiere.org.

"Interview with Garrett Brown, Inventor of the Steadicam." *FilmCrew* #16, 1997. www.steadicam.ca/mainfile/article/Garrett2/Garrett.html.

Kalmus, Herbert T., and Eleanore King Kalmus. *Mr. Technicolor.* Absecon, N.J.: MagicImage Filmbooks, 1993.

Koszarski, Richard. *An Evening's Entertainment: The Age of the Silent Feature Picture, 1915-1928.* Berkeley: University of California, 1990.

Levine, I. E. *Electronics Pioneer: Lee de Forest.* New York: Julian Messner, 1964.

Lumière, Auguste, and Louis Lumière. *Letters.* Ed. Jacques Rittaud-Hutinet. London: Faber and Faber, 1995.

MacDonnell, Kevin. *Eadweard Muybridge: The Man who Invented the Moving Picture.* Boston: Little, Brown, 1972.

Magill, Frank, ed. *The Great Scientists.* Danbury, Conn.: Grolier, 1989.

Musser, Charles. *The Emergence of Cinema: The American Screen to 1907.* Berkeley: University of California, 1990.

O'Brien, Brian, Jr. "Todd-AO: How It All Began." *In 70mm: The 70mm Newsletter,* December 1995. http://hjem.get2net.dk/in70mm/magazine/backissues/1995/42/todd_ao/toddaostory.htm.

Perham Electronics Foundation. "The Complete Lee de Forest." www.leedeforest.org.

"Polymers in Film History." www.psrc.usm.edu/macrog/macroplx/history.htm.

Puttnam, David, with Neil Watson. *Movies and Money.* New York: Knopf, 1998.

Rickitt, Richard. *Special Effects: The History and Technique.* New York: Billboard, 2000.

Samuelson, David. "Strokes of Genius." www.theasc.com/magazine/mar99/genius/index.htm.

Shorris, Sylvia, and Marion Abbott Bundy. *Talking Pictures with the People who Made Them.* New York: The New Press, 1994.

Smith, Scott. *The Film 100: A Ranking of the Most Influential People in the History of the Movies.* New York: Citadel, 1998.

Swanson, Eric. "Steadicam Frequently Asked Questions." www.kiwifilm.com/steadfaq.html.

INDEX

ABOUT THE AUTHOR

Gina De Angelis is the author of 25 books and several articles for children and young adults. She holds a bachelor's degree in theater and history and a master's degree in history, and she studies film and screenwriting in her spare time. A native of Hershey, Pennsylvania, Gina has also lived in Australia, Vermont, and Mississippi; she now lives in Virginia with her husband, daughter, gerbil, two dogs, and four guinea pigs.

PHOTO ACKNOWLEDGMENTS

Association Frères Lumière: p. 40
Fred E. Basten/Technicolor Collection: pp. 67, 69, 70, 71, 72, 73, 74
British Film Institute: pp. 82, 87
Garrett Brown: pp. 106, 113, 114, 116, 117, 118, 119
Corbis: pp. 6 (Corbis/Bettmann), 126 (Siemoneit Ronald/Corbis Sygma), 127 (Da Silva Peter/Corbis Sygma)
Dictionary of American Portraits (published by Dover Publications, Inc., 1967)**:** p. 14
Dunn Family Collection: pp. 76, 79, 85, 89, 90
Famille Lumière/Institut Lumière: cover, pp. 32, 37, 39, 42, 43

Hasbro: p. 11
Thomas Hauerslev: pp. 92, 98 (all), 101, 103, 104, back cover
Hulton/Archive by Getty Images: pp. 8, 10, 24 (top), 31, 38, 56, 105, 123
IMAX: p. 120
Library of Congress: pp. 12, 13, 18, 25, 29, 34, 46, 57, 58, 110
Perham Foundation: pp. 49, 53, 55, 60, 61
Technicolor: p. 62
U.S. Department of the Interior, National Park Service, Edison National Historic Site: pp. 16, 19, 23, 24 (bottom), 26, 35
Rick Wacha: p. 50